Beyond the Colored Coat

Dr. Bo Wagner

Beyond the Colored Coat
The Life of Joseph

Word of His Mouth Publishers
Mooresboro, NC

© 2010 Dr. Bo Wagner (Robert A. Wagner)
ISBN: 978-0-615-52048-3

Published by Word of His Mouth Publishers
Mooresboro, NC

Printed in the United States of America

All rights reserved. No part of this publication may be reproduced in any form without the prior written permission of the publisher except for quotations in printed reviews.

All Scriptures quotations are taken from the **King James Version** of the Holy Bible.

Names in this book have been changed to protect the identity of the individual.

Thank you to Chip Nuhrah for help with the cover art.

Dedication Page

This book is affectionately dedicated to my father-in-law, Don Sessions, whose life, like Joseph's, has been a remarkable journey. From Alabama farm boy, to Vietnam veteran, to Bible college, to the pastorate, followed by years on the mission field, and then years of evangelism, he has stood firm for the Lord, he has contended for the faith, he has remained true to the Word. Above all, he produced and raised a fine daughter, whom I was privileged to receive from him as my bride. He has been a friend to me and a mentor. Eternity will not be long enough for me to express properly my gratitude for all he has taught me and meant to me. He is much, much more than a father-in-law to me. So much more that I do not hesitate to say from my heart:

Here's to you, Dad.

Table of Content

Chapter	Title	Page
1	The Baby that Broke the Cycle	9
2	Large Lessons for a Little Lad	15
3	The Coat of Many Colors	25
4	Dreamer, Beautiful Dreamer	31
5	The Darkest Day	43
6	What His Brothers Could Not Take	53
7	The Puzzle Table	63
8	The Turning of the Tide	71
9	Improbable, Impossible, Par for God's Course	77
10	The Day the Stars Bowed Down	83
11	And One Is Not	89
12	Is There Any "Fun" in "Dysfunctional?"	97
13	Don't You Know?	105
14	The Rise of Judah	113
15	I Am Joseph	121
16	Dispelling the Darkness	131
17	Just the Son	137
18	A Reunion for the Ages	147
19	Honeymoon in Egypt	157
20	The Jew that Made Egypt a World Power	171
21	Daddy's Hands	183
22	Of Bones and Burials	189
	Notes	201

Chapter 1
The Baby that Broke the Cycle

Genesis 30:23 *And she conceived, and bare a son; and said, God hath taken away my reproach:* **24** *And she called his name Joseph; and said, The LORD shall add to me another son.* **25** *And it came to pass, when Rachel had born Joseph, that Jacob said unto Laban, Send me away, that I may go unto mine own place, and to my country.*

Isn't it interesting how so often you think you know people, but you just don't really know them? Especially with some of the famous names from Scripture, that really is the case. We learn about them in Sunday school, but there is only a one week lesson to tell about an entire life! How do you cover a life in thirty minutes?

What usually happens is that we learn just the one thing that person is most famous for. For instance, when you think of Daniel, it is always "Daniel in the Lion's Den." Did you know that Daniel also was made a eunuch in the king's court, yet never got bitter on God?

When you think of David, you think of "David and Goliath." Did you know that the same David that slung the rock at Goliath later had rocks thrown back at him by a man named Shimei?

When you think of Jonah, you think of "Jonah and the Whale," but what about the great prophecy of Jonah from II Kings 14?

When you think of Noah, you think of "Noah's Ark," but what about Noah and the alcohol? What about that time when Noah passed out drunk and the devastation that it brought to the family?

I could go on and on. We know just the tip of the iceberg about most of the great characters of Scripture, even though the Bible has so much more to tell of them.

Such is the case with the man Joseph. When you think of Joseph, you automatically think of Joseph and what article of clothing? The coat of many colors. Any Sunday school poster is going to show Joseph in that coat and any flannel graph will do the same. But trust me, especially with Joseph, there is so much more to tell! That is why I have entitled this book *Beyond the Colored Coat*. Joseph is one of the most in depth lives written about in the Bible. More is written of him than almost anyone other than Jesus! His life is a fascinating tapestry of color, from the black of despair, to the green of new life, and everything in between. Truly examining his life will break your heart, encourage your soul, steel your nerves, and enlighten your understanding. The colored coat is only the tip of the iceberg to this remarkable character of Scripture.

Let us begin by looking at "The Baby that Broke the Cycle."

Before we begin looking at this passage, let me make you aware of one thing you will need to keep in mind every step of the way throughout this book -- Joseph is one of the most complete pictures of the Lord Jesus Christ you will ever see in the Bible. All through the Old Testament, God was painting pictures of what Jesus was going to be like, and when He got around to Joseph, He painted a really close picture!

Joseph was the father's prized son, just as Jesus is His Father's prized Son.

Joseph was clothed in a very special garment, just as Jesus was clothed in a scarlet robe in which to be crucified.

Joseph's garment was later dipped in blood, and Jesus will come back in a garment dipped in blood in Revelation 19.

Joseph was sold by those closest to him for the price in silver of a common slave. Jesus was also sold by Judas, a man He called friend, for the price in silver of a common slave.

Joseph was imprisoned and suffered unjustly, just as Jesus was imprisoned and suffered unjustly.

Joseph's sufferings were for the good of the entire world, which he saved from a famine. Jesus' sufferings were for the good of the entire world, which He came to save from sin.

Joseph came through all of his troubles to end up seated at the right hand of Pharaoh. Jesus came through all of His troubles to end up seated at the right hand of the Father.

When you see Joseph, you are seeing a forerunner in type of Jesus Himself. So let's start looking at this remarkable life.

The Heritage of Joseph

The story of Joseph really begins in Genesis 12 with his great-grandfather Abraham. God reached down into Ur of the Chaldees and chose Abraham to be the father of a nation. He sent Abraham, known then as Abram, into what would later be the Promised Land for the Children of Israel. Abraham would wander that land as a stranger, knowing that God would one day give it to his descendants. This was a remarkable act of faith on Abraham's part. Abraham went, not knowing where he was going, simply because God said, "Go!" That type of faith would later be evident running through the veins of his great-grandson Joseph, who always believed what he could not see, simply because he judged God faithful Who had promised it.

Abraham's son, Isaac, was the next step in the lineage of Joseph. God bypassed the child of the flesh, Ishmael, and chose the child of the promise, Isaac. Isaac himself later became a type of Christ, being taken to Mount Moriah in Genesis 22 as a sacrifice for sin. God spared his life that day, but two thousand or so years later, on that same spot, God the Father would send His own Son, Jesus Christ, to die for our sins.

Since Isaac came down from the mountaintop alive, he was later able to bear a son named Jacob. Jacob did not have quite the level of godly character that Abraham had, perhaps not even that of Isaac. His name means *supplanter* or *trickster*. His life was marked by deception and guile, interspersed with moments of godliness. He was inconsistent, mixed, unstable, good, and bad depending on the circumstances, and his children inherited that mixture. Some of them ended up mirroring his some-times-godliness, and many of them ended up mirroring his often-times-deceitfulness.

This is the great-grandfather, the grandfather, and the father of Joseph; this is his heritage. It is in the heritage given by his father, Jacob, that we find the immediate context and flavor of Joseph's life. Jacob had been battling with his own brother, Esau, from the womb. Jacob had twice tricked him, and in fear for his life because of it, had to leave home. He and his mother, who had orchestrated the last deception, intended for the parting to be brief, just long enough for Esau to cool down. But the parting ended up being twenty years, and Jacob never saw his mother alive again. Oh, the high cost and unexpected consequences of sin!

Jacob, for his part, found himself in a far land, the land of his mother's people. He went to work for his Uncle Laban, his mother's brother. Part of his motivation was his need for employment, but the bigger thing that kept him there was a pretty young thing named Rachel! Rachel, Laban's daughter, was the most beautiful thing Jacob ever laid eyes on. He set about to marry her, and the purchase price for her dowry was seven years of hard labor! Yet Jacob gladly paid the price, for the great love that he had for Rachel. But then, (Oh Jacob, could you not have foreseen that the law of sowing and reaping would catch up with you eventually?) the unthinkable happened. On the wedding night, Laban, who would prove to be even more skilled of a con-man than Jacob, slipped his (let's be kind and try to avoid the words "hideously ugly") less attractive daughter, Leah, over on Jacob. Jacob, when all was said and done, ended up with two wives instead of one, which is always a great recipe for trouble.

Nonetheless, these two women, along with their handmaidens, Zilpah and Bilhah, combined to produce for Jacob twelve sons and a daughter named Dinah. One of those sons is the subject of our study, the remarkable man named Joseph.

The Hope of Joseph

Genesis 30:23 *And she conceived, and bare a son; and said, God hath taken away my reproach:* **24** *And she called his* *name Joseph; and said, The LORD shall add to me another son.* **25** *And it came to pass, when Rachel had born Joseph, that Jacob said unto Laban, Send me away, that I may go unto mine own place, and to my country.*

By the time of Joseph's arrival in this world, the immediate family around him was obviously in a bad cycle. They had fallen far from the heights of godly Abraham. But this simple child, this precious baby, broke the cycle of everyone around him.

Consider first of all the woman Rachel, Jacob's favorite wife, Joseph's mother. This young woman, up to this point, was in the worst position possible for a Jewish wife. Her life was utterly meaningless, because she had been unable to have children! Complicating the matter was the fact that her own sister, her husband's other wife, had been able to bear children. This caused a fairly heated family conflict.

Genesis 30:1 *And when Rachel saw that she bare Jacob no children, Rachel envied her sister; and said unto Jacob, Give me children, or else I die.* **2** *And Jacob's anger was kindled against Rachel: and he said, Am I in God's stead, who hath withheld from thee the fruit of the womb?*

When baby Joseph came into Rachel's life, her life finally had meaning.

Genesis 30:23 *And she conceived, and bare a son; and said, God hath taken away my reproach:*

What a gift from God was the precious child Joseph to his needy mother Rachel! And yet, one cannot help but wonder, what pressure that must place on a child, growing up knowing that a parent's life has no meaning apart from him! Today's parents will hopefully find their meaning for life in God and husband rather than viewing life as meaningless apart from children.

When this baby came into Rachel's life, she also started to look toward the future. This was a radical breaking of the cycle for a woman who was immersed in the agony of the present.

Genesis 30:24 *And she called his name Joseph; and said, The LORD shall add to me another son.*

The Scripture gives us no indication that God told Rachel she would have another son, but since He had given her

Joseph, she was already looking ahead to future blessings from God. Having received good at His hand once, she confidently looked toward the future anticipating more.

And what of Jacob? Joseph broke a negative cycle for him as well. When this baby came into Jacob's life, he started to desire his true homeland.

Genesis 30:25 *And it came to pass, when Rachel had born Joseph, that Jacob said unto Laban, Send me away, that I may go unto mine own place, and to my country.*

For a time, despite the hardships, Jacob had settled down and grown somewhat comfortable in a land that was not his own. Having this child come into his life gave him a longing for home.

Oh, what a phenomenal picture of Christ Joseph thus becomes! When a person receives the Son of God into his heart, a strange thing happens. The world around him, so comfortable and familiar for so long, seems to suddenly dim and diminish. The heart begins to stir, and it is as if he can smell the sweet air of Emmanuel's land and recognize it as his own. The songs of Earth begin to be drowned out by the singing from a far distant shore; the pleasures of Earth seem to become worthless trinkets and baubles. The bed is still soft and family still sweet, but the beckoning call of Heaven grows stronger day by day, until finally, he closes his physical eyes here, blinks once or twice, and finds himself staring into the pure eyes of the Son of God, Who first began to stir his heart with a desire for Home.

Chapter 2
Large Lessons for a Little Lad

Genesis 33:1 *And Jacob lifted up his eyes, and looked, and, behold, Esau came, and with him four hundred men. And he divided the children unto Leah, and unto Rachel, and unto the two handmaids.* **2** *And he put the handmaids and their children foremost, and Leah and her children after, and Rachel and Joseph hindermost.* **3** *And he passed over before them, and bowed himself to the ground seven times, until he came near to his brother.* **4** *And Esau ran to meet him, and embraced him, and fell on his neck, and kissed him: and they wept.* **5** *And he lifted up his eyes, and saw the women and the children; and said, Who are those with thee? And he said, The children which God hath graciously given thy servant.* **6** *Then the handmaidens came near, they and their children, and they bowed themselves.* **7** *And Leah also with her children came near, and bowed themselves: and after came Joseph near and Rachel, and they bowed themselves.* **8** *And he said, What meanest thou by all this drove which I met? And he said, These are to find grace in the sight of my lord.* **9** *And Esau said, I have enough, my brother; keep that thou hast unto thyself.* **10** *And Jacob said, Nay, I pray thee, if now I have found grace in thy sight, then receive my present at my hand: for therefore I have seen thy face, as though I had seen the face of God, and thou wast pleased with me.* **11** *Take, I pray thee, my blessing that is brought to thee; because God hath dealt graciously with me, and because I have enough. And he urged him, and he took it.* **12** *And he said, Let* *us take our journey, and let us go, and I will go before thee.* **13** *And he said unto him, My lord knoweth that the children are tender, and the flocks and herds with young are with me: and if men should overdrive them one day, all the flock will die.* **14** *Let my lord, I pray thee, pass over before his servant: and I will lead on softly, according as the cattle that goeth before me and the children be able to endure, until I come unto my lord unto Seir.* **15** *And Esau said, Let me now leave with thee some of the folk that are with me. And he said, What needeth it? let me find grace in the sight of my lord.* **16** *So Esau returned that day on his way unto Seir.* **17** *And Jacob journeyed to Succoth, and built him an house, and made booths for his cattle: therefore the name of the place is called Succoth.* **18** *And Jacob came to Shalem, a city of Shechem, which is in the land of Canaan, when he came from Padanaram; and pitched his tent before the city.* **19** *And he bought a parcel of a field, where he had spread his tent, at the hand of the children of Hamor, Shechem's father, for an hundred pieces of money.* **20** *And he erected there an altar, and called it Elelohe-Israel.*

There are times you look at an adult, think back to their childhood, and think it's no wonder they turned out so well. Their mom and dad were both godly, sensible, down to earth folks. He/she turned out just like them. But then there are the other times. You know, the times when you look at someone who has turned out so very well and think, how on earth did that guy turn out so well? How is he not a stark raving lunatic? How has she not turned out to be a bitter old hag like her momma? How did that guy not end up behind bars like his worthless daddy? How did that lady not end up etc. etc. etc.

Let me tell you someone who was like that. Joseph was like that. When you stop and think of his lying father and needy mother, how on earth did he turn out to be such a rock-solid man for God? Even while he was young, he was seeing people that would do right one minute and then wrong the next. Take for instance the account we just read. Do you know how old Joseph was at this time? He was six years old. As a six year old little boy, he was seeing things both good and bad that could have shaped him for life.

Let me give you a little background to bring you up to speed. In the last chapter we looked at the birth of Joseph and how it changed so much in his family.

After Joseph was born, Jacob wanted to go back to his homeland, but Laban didn't want him to go. Laban saw how good of a shepherd Jacob was, so he hired him to stick around and keep his sheep. He had already been there for fourteen years working for Rachel and Leah, and he stayed six more years working as a shepherd, with his wages being whichever of the sheep were born a certain color or skin type. During those six years, Jacob got rich off of Laban's sheep, and Laban started getting pretty angry about it.

So Jacob decided to run. Without telling a soul, he packed up his family and possessions and took off.

Three days later, Laban found out about it and hit the roof. He chased Jacob down; they had a nasty falling out and then went their separate ways for good.

In chapter 32, Jacob sent some messengers out to make contact with his brother Esau. If you will remember, the last time these two were in the same place Jacob had been so dishonest and sneaky towards his brother that Esau determined to kill him. As far as Jacob knew, twenty years later, Esau was still holding a grudge.

So, knowing that Esau would hear of his coming, he sent messengers ahead to talk to Esau and feel him out to see if he was going to be safe or not. When the messengers got back, they said, "We met up with Esau. He's coming to see you. He has four hundred men with him." That brings us up to our text where little Joseph got to see and learn so many things.

Good Lesson: A Problem Left Unresolved Only Gets Bigger with Time

Genesis 33:1a *And Jacob lifted up his eyes, and looked, and, behold, Esau came, and with him four hundred men...*

Four hundred men. Would you say that is a big problem or a VERY big problem? But you know what? It didn't start as a four hundred to one problem. It started a lot smaller twenty years before this.

Genesis 27:41 *And Esau hated Jacob because of the blessing wherewith his father blessed him: and Esau said in his* heart, *The days of mourning for my father are at hand; then will I slay my brother Jacob.*

Notice that pronoun *I*? When this whole issue started, it was a one-to-one problem. That problem went unresolved for twenty years. Jacob ran from the problem for twenty years. Twenty years later it was a four hundred-to-one problem.

That is the way things work when you leave problems unresolved! A family knows they have financial problems, but they don't want to know just how bad their situation really is. So they refuse to answer the phone, throw away collection notices, and take vacations, on credit, to relieve the stress.

A family has marital problems, and the wife says, "We need some help, let's get some godly counseling for this." But Mr. Proud husband says, "I don't want anyone to know we are struggling; that would embarrass me."

A parent is raising a child with obvious behavioral problems and saying, "Oh, he/she is just being a kid. Kids do that; no need to worry. Kids are going to be mean to animals; no need to worry. Kids are going to lie a little; no need to worry."

Joseph knew better. Joseph learned a lesson about not leaving problems unresolved, and later on in life that lesson saved the world. Remember that time later in Egypt when there were seven years of prosperity followed by seven years of famine? Joseph didn't wait for the famine to get bad before he finally did something. He didn't even wait for the famine to start before he did something; he started dealing with the problem seven years before the problem even started. That is getting a jump on the problem!

What a great lesson little Joseph learned: a problem unresolved only gets bigger with time.

Bad Lesson: I'm Better than Everyone Else
Genesis 33:1b *And he divided the children unto Leah, and unto Rachel, and unto the two handmaids.* **2** *And he put the handmaids and their children foremost, and Leah and her children after, and Rachel and Joseph hindermost.*

I wonder, how would you feel if you were the kids and the women in the front of that line? Let me show you something. You might automatically think that Jacob did this by age, sending them from oldest to youngest. He didn't. The very first four kids he had were by Leah: Reuben, Simeon, Levi, and Judah. Then he started having kids by Rachel's handmaid. But when it came time to send them into danger, the younger kids, the kids of the two handmaids Bilhah and Zilpah were in the front of the line! The older kids of Leah came after them, and then came Joseph last of all. In other words, Jacob arranged them according to which ones he liked the best!

That trend continued throughout these boys' lives. Do you remember that coat of many colors that came along eleven years later? That was given to Joseph specifically because daddy liked him best. Is it any wonder the other kids hated him? Jacob may as well have put a "kick me" sign on Joseph's back.

That lesson is one that we can all be grateful Joseph decided not to learn. If he had really bought into this idea that he was better than everybody else, can you imagine how different his life story would have turned out?

Why shouldn't I sleep with Potiphar's wife? Who does Potiphar think he is, anyway? I'm Joseph; I'm better than him!

Why should I help these two prisoners that are having these bad dreams? That's their problem. I'm Joseph; I'm better than them.

The entire world is starving? Who cares? If they didn't have the sense to prepare for this famine, tough. At least there's food on my table; that's all that really matters.

Thank God, Joseph overcame this terrible lesson that his daddy taught him. If you want to ruin children for life, there is hardly a better way to do it than to teach them they are better than everybody else. Teach them that no one ever has the right to call them down. Teach them that if they want something, somebody has to give it to them. Teach them that they are prettier, smarter, of more worth than the other "little brats" around them. If you can do all that, you will produce a kid that no one can stand, but that will be okay with them, they will have already figured out that it is everybody else's problem, not theirs.

We have tried to teach our kids early, "The universe does not revolve around you!" There used to be a child at our church that we called "The Precious." That kid had learned this bad lesson very well. "The Precious" could not be called down, by anyone, without momma and daddy running to baby's rescue and pointing out that everyone else was the problem. "The Precious: could commit the most heinous of sins, and, when caught, turn on the tear-faucets and remove all consequences of the offending actions. "The Precious" was favored over other siblings, other church kids, and, truthfully, over God.

Do not ever let your kids think they are better than everyone else!

Good Lesson: Life Is too Short to Hold Grudges
Genesis 33:3 And he passed over before them, and bowed himself to the ground seven times, until he came near to his brother. 4 And Esau ran to meet him, and embraced him, and fell on his neck, and kissed him: and they wept.

Have you paid attention to who taught this lesson? For all of his flaws, for all of his wickedness, Esau got at least this one thing right. It was Esau that ran to meet Jacob; it was Esau that embraced him; it was Esau that kissed Jacob.

I don't know exactly at what point it happened, but at some time during those twenty years, Esau gave up that grudge he had been holding. I suspect from what I read that it was while he was on the way to meet him. I suspect that this four hundred man clan started as a war party and somewhere along the way turned to a welcome home party.

What a lesson Joseph learned on this one! Can you think of a similar situation later in his own life? Some little thing about his own brothers trying to kill him, then selling him into slavery, then him later having the power to end their lives and not doing it? He learned this as a six year old little boy.

Life is too short to hold grudges!

Good Lesson: A Little Manners Go a Long Way
Genesis 33:5 And he lifted up his eyes, and saw the women and the children; and said, Who are those with thee? And he said, The children which God hath graciously given thy servant. 6 Then the handmaidens came near, they and their children, and they bowed themselves. 7 And Leah also with her children came near, and bowed themselves: and after came Joseph near and Rachel, and they bowed themselves.

Do we not live in the rudest generation ever? Children call adults by their first names, they respond with "Huh?" or "What?" or "Yeah" when asked a question, and the words "Sir" or "Ma'am" are never heard from their lips. An elderly person will walk up to talk to a sitting youth, and the youth remains seated rather than standing, as is commanded by Leviticus 19:32. Conversations are held without a person ever looking the other in the eyes. Interrupting is a habitual practice. A parent scolds a child, only to have the child respond with an insolent, "Whatever."

This, by the way, is exactly what happens to a generation when children are spoiled rather than spanked! In Jacob's generation, rudeness was not tolerated, and even in a crooked man like Jacob, good manners were evident. As Esau the elder brother came to meet him, everyone in the family bowed before him.

Joseph learned this lesson, and it served him well. Think of his manners concerning Potiphar, the prison keeper, and Pharaoh himself! In all situations, Joseph showed himself to be a person of good manners. Humanly speaking, that contributed mightily to his rise to power.

Bad Lesson: You Can Buy Your Way Out of Trouble
Genesis 33:8 *And he said, What meanest thou by all this drove which I met? And he said, These are to find grace in the sight of my lord.* **9** *And Esau said, I have enough, my brother; keep that thou hast unto thyself.* **10** *And Jacob said, Nay, I pray thee, if now I have found grace in thy sight, then receive my present at my hand: for therefore I have seen thy face, as though I had seen the face of God, and thou wast pleased with me.* **11** *Take, I pray thee, my blessing that is brought to thee; because God hath dealt graciously with me, and because I have enough. And he urged him, and he took it.*

Jacob had spent his life as a con-artist, but to give him credit, he was at least a hard working con-artist, and he became a fairly wealthy man. So, when confronted with a possibly homicidal elder brother, Jacob's solution was obvious, at least to him. Rather than apologize for previous wrongs, he simply bought his way out of trouble!

It is good that Joseph never appropriated this bad lesson, because for all the years that he had such trouble, he never had any money or power or influence with which to buy his way out of trouble! He just had to rely on always doing right. Not surprisingly, Joseph's approach worked much better than that of his father, Jacob.

This, surely, is another good way to ruin your kids, be sure and always buy their way out of trouble! We had a family in the early years of our church with an older son who was bent on trouble. He defied every form of authority, and as a result, often found himself in trouble with the law. One day, his long-suffering mother called the office to speak to me. She explained that her son had gotten in trouble with the law again, this time for selling drugs. Lots of them. He was in jail and facing very significant prison time. He had asked her and his father to put their house up as collateral so that he could get out of jail on bond while awaiting trial. I "calmly" said: "ARE YOU NUTS?!? WHY ARE YOU EVEN CONSIDERING THIS?!? YOUR BOY IS GOING TO SKIP BAIL, LEAVE TOWN, GO INTO HIDING, AND YOU WILL LOSE YOUR HOUSE! DON'T DO IT!"

She said, "I can't leave my boy in jail, Preacher!" Which to me begs the question, if you already had your mind made up, then why did you even call to ask my advice? If you would like, dear reader, come to see me at my church some time. We will get into my car, and I will drive you about three miles from my church, where sits a once beautiful home that another family now lives in, and has ever since a rotten kid skipped bail and cost his dumb-as-dirt parents their home.

Bad Lesson: When the Heat Is Off, Go Back to Your Old Ways

Genesis 33:12 And he said, Let us take our journey, and let us go, and I will go before thee. 13 And he said unto him, My lord knoweth that the children are tender, and the flocks and herds with young are with me: and if men should overdrive them one day, all the flock will die. 14 Let my lord, I pray thee, pass over before his servant: and I will lead on softly, according as the cattle that goeth before me and the children be able to endure, until I come unto my lord unto Seir. 15 And

Esau said, Let me now leave with thee some of the folk that are with me. And he said, What needeth it? let me find grace in the sight of my lord. **16** *So Esau returned that day on his way unto Seir.* **17** *And Jacob journeyed to Succoth, and built him an house, and made booths for his cattle: therefore the name of the place is called Succoth.* **18** *And Jacob came to Shalem, a city of Shechem, which is in the land of Canaan, when he came from Padanaram; and pitched his tent before the city.*

Let me explain the geography behind this point. When Jacob fled from Laban, he was running from a place called Padan Aram. That was just about due north from where Esau was in Mount Seir. So Jacob was heading south from Padan Aram, and Esau was heading north from Mount Seir, and they met at the Brook Penuel. Jacob had come about 180 miles south, Esau had come roughly 90 miles north.

After they "reconciled," Esau said, "Ok, baby brother, let's go back to my place. You've called me lord; you've said I am in charge, so come on back with me." Jacob said, "I will! But you go ahead of me. I have these little kids, Joey here especially, I have all these flocks, I need to go a lot slower than you. So you go ahead, I'll catch up." Esau said, "Ok, but I'll leave some of my folks behind with you to help you on your way to my place." Jacob said, "There's no need for that. Let me find grace in thy sight, you just go on ahead, I promise I'll be right behind you."

So Esau loaded up and headed back due south toward Mount Seir. But Jacob didn't. In fact, he never even took a single step in that direction! Jacob turned due west, crossed over the Jordan River, and finally stopped in a place called Shechem, which "coincidentally" put 120 miles, the Dead Sea, and the Judaean Mountains between himself and Esau!

Can you imagine the conversation between Jacob and little six year old Joseph? "I thought we were going to Mount Seir with Uncle Esau, Daddy." "Hush, Son, you're too young to understand these things." Once again, thank God that Joseph chose not to follow in the negative lessons of his father! Through good times and bad, he maintained a consistent and godly character.

Good Lesson: Get What You Get Honestly

Genesis 33:19 *And he bought a parcel of a field, where he had spread his tent, at the hand of the children of Hamor, Shechem's father, for an hundred pieces of money.*

There are some miracles in Scripture that are so obvious, everyone recognizes them.

The parting of the Red Sea...
The feeding of the five thousand...
The walking on water...
Raising Lazarus from the dead...

But, friend, as great as those miracles are, I am inclined to think that they don't begin to compare with the miracle in this verse: ***Jacob actually bought and paid for something instead of conning his way into it!***

This is the same guy that put animal skins on his arms, changed his voice, went into his blind old daddy's room, and pretended to be his brother and stole the blessing! This is the same guy that "just happened" to be cooking a delicious meal right at the moment his brother came in famished from the field so he could use his brother's hunger to get his birthright. This is the guy that somehow managed to get the stronger sheep of Laban to produce his colored sheep and the weaker ones to produce Laban's color of sheep. Everywhere he ever went, he was the world's biggest con-artist. And here he is whipping out actual money to buy something!

Good Lesson: Our God Is the Mighty God

Genesis 33:20 *And he erected there an altar, and called it Elelohe-Israel.*

This name means "God, the Mighty God of Israel." Of all of the lessons little Joseph learned, this was perhaps the most valuable. From the pit, to Potiphar's house, to the prison, to the palace, Joseph never once relied on his own strength but always and only on the strength of God. What a radical departure from the way of his father, who cheated, conned, connived, and cajoled his way into most every situation!

Chapter 3
The Coat of Many Colors

Genesis 37:1 *And Jacob dwelt in the land wherein his father was a stranger, in the land of Canaan.* **2** *These are the generations of Jacob. Joseph, being seventeen years old, was feeding the flock with his brethren; and the lad was with the sons of Bilhah, and with the sons of Zilpah, his father's wives: and Joseph brought unto his father their evil report.* **3** *Now Israel loved Joseph more than all his children, because he was the son of his old age: and he made him a coat of many colours.* **4** *And when his brethren saw that their father loved him more than all his brethren, they hated him, and could not speak peaceably unto him.*

I love the sayings of old-timers. "Good Lord willin' and the creek don't rise." "Way down yonder in the Paw-Paw patch." (Dear Old-Timers, could one of you please contact this young pup and tell me what exactly a Paw Paw patch is?) "Set a spell."

Another one I love is "The clothes make the man." That came from the time (a much better time, I think) when men wore suits and fedora hats and ladies carried parasols. The idea was that if you dressed for success, you would be successful; you were who you dressed like. I like that old saying, but unfortunately, it isn't really true!

My mom used to have an old Smothers Brothers record (for people even younger than myself, let me explain that a "record" is a big round plastic thing that makes scratchy sounding music when put on an ancient device called a "turn table") and there was a song on it that goes like this:

> As I walked out on the streets of Laredo, as I walked out in Laredo one day, I saw a young cowboy all dressed in white linen, all dressed in white linen, as cold as the clay.
>
> I see by your outfit, that you are a cowboy, I see by your outfit that you're a cowboy too, we see by our outfits that we are both cowboys, if you get an outfit you can be a cowboy too!

That was a sarcastic and effective way of saying that even though you should always dress right, clothes don't really make the man or the woman! I can put on cleats and shoulder pads, and it still won't make me an NFL linebacker (except maybe for the Miami Dolphins). Billy can put on a tux and shiny shoes, and it still won't make him a ball room dancer. Jane can put on a hideous pantsuit and learn to cackle, and it still won't make her Hillary Clinton.

Clothes may be a *reflection* of who you are, but they do not *determine* who you are.

But the young man we are studying, Joseph, could have come closer than anyone to claiming that clothes do make the man. One piece of clothing in particular changed his entire life. This is the thing for which Joseph is the most famous. This book on Joseph is called *Beyond the Colored Coat*, because there is much more to his life than this one incident. But this chapter is about that famous piece of clothing, so it is entitled "The Coat of Many Colors." Let me quickly bring you up to speed on Joseph.

Remember that Joseph was the baby that broke the cycle. He was the son of his father's old age, the son of Jacob's beloved wife, Rachel. A lot of things changed when he was born.

When he was all of six years old, he was there when his father re-met his brother Esau, who had been determined for twenty years to kill him. As a six year old boy, Joseph learned a lot of good lessons and a lot of bad lessons during that tense meeting. Those lessons would shape the way he made decisions throughout the rest of his life.

From there, he and his family moved to Shalem, a city in a place called Shechem. It was there that his older brothers Simeon and Levi murdered a bunch of helpless men.

After that incident, Jacob, in Genesis 35, moved all of the family to Bethel. From there, they started heading towards what would later be known as Bethlehem. It was on that trip that tragedy struck for little Joseph. His mother, Rachel, went into labor with Joseph's little brother, Benjamin, and died while giving birth. They went from there to Hebron where Jacob was re-united with his old father, Isaac.

That brings us up to chapter 37, and the account of the many colored coat.

A Patient Waiting
   Genesis 37:1 *And Jacob dwelt in the land wherein his father was a stranger, in the land of Canaan.*

This land, all of it, had already been promised to Abraham, Isaac, Jacob, all of their family. Yet here they are, as strangers in it. Many of the promises of God are gained only by patient waiting. The book of Hebrews makes a statement about the family of Abraham that would be considered heart-breaking to some.

   Hebrews 11:13 *These all died in faith, not having received the promises, but having seen them afar off, and were persuaded of them, and embraced them, and confessed that they were strangers and pilgrims on the earth.*

Abraham knew that he and his immediate family would not receive the promises themselves but that their descendants several generations down the line would. Abraham, Isaac, Jacob, and Joseph all died without owning more than a small sliver of land in Canaan. So the account of Joseph is one in which, though he possessed a colored coat, he possessed very little else in the Land of Promise!

A Persistent Watching

Genesis 37:2 *These are the generations of Jacob. Joseph, being seventeen years old, was feeding the flock with his brethren; and the lad was with the sons of Bilhah, and with the sons of Zilpah, his father's wives: and Joseph brought unto his father their evil report.*

My children were taught a catchy little jingle by a family member in my church: "Tattle tale, Ginger Ale, stick your head in a garbage pail!" Now, I must confess that I fail to see why Ginger Ale has been unceremoniously dragged into all of this mess. It seems like a perfectly delightful beverage ill befitting either tattlers or garbage cans. Nonetheless, sticking the head of tattlers in a garbage can, that part I do understand! No one likes a tattle-tale.

But Joseph was not "tattling!" The reputation of the father was on the line, and the other brothers had already demonstrated their ability to be ruinously wicked. He was simply obeying his father's wishes and monitoring people who desperately needed it. Unfortunately, parents, older siblings do not take kindly to being "monitored" by younger siblings. We put younger kids in a terrible situation when we make them do that! And with Joseph, it nearly cost him his life.

A Precious Weaving

Genesis 37:3 *Now Israel loved Joseph more than all his children, because he was the son of his old age: and he made him a coat of many colours.*

The coats of Joseph's day were most always made from wool, which ranges in color from white to light gray. That lent it well to the ability to be dyed. In order to make a coat of many colors, individual patches of the fabric were dyed and then woven together. It was a time consuming, expensive process. By giving Joseph this coat, Jacob was announcing to the world how much he thought of his son.

But the other brothers were not naked, they had clothing as well. Simple, wool, white to gray clothing.

This coat was precious, offensive, and dangerous. It was precious to Jacob, offensive to the other sons, and dangerous to Joseph. It made him more of a marked man than ever. It let the jealous brothers see him from a long way off and gave them time to discuss among themselves how much they hated him. It was a visible, tangible reminder that their father did not love them as much as he loved Joseph. It was a sure sign of favoritism, and favoritism has ever been a deadly toxin within families.

But on another level, this coat is one more thing that serves as a reminder of how the Father feels about the Son:

Philippians 2:9 *Wherefore God also hath highly exalted him, and given him a name which is above every name: **10** That at the name of Jesus every knee should bow, of things in heaven, and things in earth, and things under the earth; **11** And that every tongue should confess that Jesus Christ is Lord, to the glory of God the Father.*

We, who are saved, are all *sons* of God, but Jesus is THE SON of God, His Beloved, His One and Only. The brother's legacy was determined largely by what they did with Joseph; our eternity will be determined entirely by what we do with Jesus!

A Perverse Wasting

Genesis 37:4 *And when his brethren saw that their father loved him more than all his brethren, they hated him, and could not speak peaceably unto him.*

It is interesting to note the direction of the brothers' hatred. What did Joseph do? Nothing. The verb in this verse is directed to the father, Jacob. Jacob did something; Jacob loved Joseph more than the other brothers. But when the brothers chose a spot towards which to direct their hatred, they chose to direct it not towards Jacob but towards Joseph. They descended to such a depth of jealousy that they "could not speak peaceably unto him." When it came time to pass the corn flakes around the table in the morning, the brothers had something hateful to say to Joseph. When they started off for work, they had something hateful to say to Joseph. When it came time for a break in the afternoon, they had something hateful to say to Joseph. When they met at the well to quench their thirst, they had something hateful to say to Joseph. When they washed their hands at the end of the day, they had something hateful to say to Joseph. When they gathered for the evening meal, they had something hateful to say to Joseph. Before they went to sleep for the night, they had something hateful to say to Joseph.

What a waste! Every moment lost in that type of anger and jealousy is a moment that can never be regained. Family members in our day often go for years without even speaking to each other over some small slight from the past. Church members sit on opposite sides of the church, if they even still come, because of a (probably unintentional to begin with) hurtful comment from bygone days. Husbands and wives split a home, leaving the kids to pick up the shattered pieces in juvenile dust-pans ill-equipped for the job because neither would forgive.

Joseph's brothers fumed, fussed, fretted, and, finally, betrayed their own brother. They went for who knows how long without even being able to speak a peaceable word to him, then they sold him into slavery, and nearly made their father, whose love they claimed to covet, die of a broken heart. Over what? A fancy piece of clothing.

Chapter 4
Dreamer, Beautiful Dreamer

Genesis 37:5 *And Joseph dreamed a dream, and he told it his brethren: and they hated him yet the more.* **6** *And he said unto them, Hear, I pray you, this dream which I have dreamed:* **7** *For, behold, we were binding sheaves in the field, and, lo, my sheaf arose, and also stood upright; and, behold, your sheaves stood round about, and made obeisance to my sheaf.* **8** *And his brethren said to him, Shalt thou indeed reign over us? or shalt thou indeed have dominion over us? And they hated him yet the more for his dreams, and for his words.* **9** *And he dreamed yet another dream, and told it his brethren, and said, Behold, I have dreamed a dream more; and, behold, the sun and the moon and the eleven stars made obeisance to me.* **10** *And he told it to his father, and to his brethren: and his father rebuked him, and said unto him, What is this dream that thou hast dreamed? Shall I and thy mother and thy brethren indeed come to bow down ourselves to thee to the earth?* **11** *And his brethren envied him; but his father observed the saying.*

There is a popular lullaby song written by a man named Stephen Foster. It was first published in the year he died, which was 1864. That sweet little song goes like this:

> Beautiful dreamer, wake unto me,
> Starlight and dewdrops are waiting for thee;
> Sounds of the rude world, heard in the day,
> Lull'd by the moonlight have all pass'd away!

Beautiful dreamer, queen of my song,
List while I woo thee with soft melody,
Gone are the cares of life's busy throng,
Beautiful dreamer, awake unto me!
Beautiful dreamer, awake unto me!

Beautiful dreamer, out on the sea
Mermaids are chanting the wild Lorelie;
Over the streamlet vapors are borne,
Waiting to fade at the bright coming morn.

Beautiful dreamer, beam on my heart,
E'en as the morn on the streamlet and sea;
Then will all clouds of sorrow depart,
Beautiful dreamer, awake unto me!
Beautiful dreamer, awake unto me!

Whoever Stephen Foster was, he had nothing at all in common with the brothers of Joseph. As far as they were concerned, their little dreamer could drop dead, and they wouldn't miss him!

We're looking at the life of Joseph. There is so much more to his life than just the episode with the coat of many colors. Let's call this particular dreamy episode "Dreamer, Beautiful Dreamer."

An Irrational Hatred

Genesis 37:5 *And Joseph dreamed a dream, and he told it his brethren: and they hated him yet the more.*

I know that we are supposed to "love" even our enemies, but I suspect that it is possible, if you look hard enough, to find some decent reasons not to "like" people.

Once upon a time, the Miami Dolphins actually had a pretty good team. In fact, there was a time back during the Dan Marino years when they were great. One year in particular, they were playing the Colts to see who would continue on into the playoffs. I was over at a friend's house on Sunday afternoon and we were watching it. The problem was his uncle Bud had the remote control. Now Bud knew how much this game meant to me, which is what made all that happened next so abominable. The Dolphins were driving, they got down to the ten, and Marino lobbed a pass into the end zone. What happened? I'm not really sure, because in mid-flight Uncle Bud changed the channel. This continued on for the next two hours. Every time a significant play happened he changed the channel in mid-play, waited a minute or so, and changed it back. I hate to admit it, but since that day I have changed the last consonant in his name from a "d" to a "double t" whenever I refer to him.

It is logical, rational, and perfectly understandable to dislike someone like that (I'm just kidding, please put down the pen and paper and refrain from writing me that hate mail). But please consider the irrational hatred of Joseph's brothers. They didn't "dislike" him; they hated him with a bitter, murderous hatred. Why? Because he dreamed a dream!

You husbands out there, I wonder if any of you are brave enough to admit if this has happened to you, as it has to me. I can remember on more than one occasion my dear, rational, logical, college-educated wife would be acting strangely cold towards me in the morning. I would say, 'Honey, what's wrong?" She would respond, "Nothing." That would go on for a while until finally, she would just about blow a gasket and say, "Do you know what you did last night?" Ignorant, I would respond, "Uh, did I steal the covers again?" To which I would be told, "No. I dreamed that you had an affair with some little hussy!" And I would say, "Wait a minute! Are you actually telling me that you're angry at me for something that you dreamed I did?" Has anybody but me ever had that happen?

How insane is it to get mad over a dream? Joseph's brothers were ready to kill him over a dream he had!

May I stop and be very practical for a few minutes? This is, after all, a very practical book. I am amazed at the tiny, little, insignificant things that people get mad at each other over:

"So and so didn't shake my hand" is a pretty sorry reason to get mad at someone.

I actually had a preacher get mad at me for not calling on him to pray during one of our revival meetings! It must have been the direction of the Lord, because a person like that probably can't get a prayer through anyway!

I've known husbands to be ready to walk out on a wife because the house was messy.

I've seen kids who had been friends for years stop talking to each other over a boy or a girl.

I've known wives furious with their husbands over girls they dated before they ever met!

May I give you some good advice? Don't be a moron. Don't lose an IQ contest to a bag of hair. If you're going to be mad at someone, there better be a really big, really rational reason for it, and then you better learn to forgive for your own good!

This was an irrational hatred.

An Irresponsible Choice

Genesis 37:6 *And he said unto them, Hear, I pray you, this dream which I have dreamed: 7 For, behold, we were binding sheaves in the field, and, lo, my sheaf arose, and also stood upright; and, behold, your sheaves stood round about, and made obeisance to my sheaf.*

There are so many good things you can say about Joseph. Joseph was honest... Joseph was persistent... Joseph was hard working... But at this point in his life, you would also have to honestly say that Joseph wasn't the brightest bulb in the box!

How smart is it, knowing that your brothers are insanely jealous of you, to say, "Hey guys, guess what? I dreamed that all of you are going to bow down to me!" I bet that went over real well. How many of you older brothers or older sisters would react well to that?

Everyone in those days understood that God at that time used dreams to tell people of the future. They regarded this as Joseph prophesying that they would all bow to him.

The thing is, Joseph should have known that they would react to it this way. Just because God gave him this dream didn't mean that he had to go tell his brothers. This really was an irresponsible choice.

Proverbs 29:11 *A fool uttereth all his mind: but a wise man keepeth it in till afterwards.*

How much simpler life would be if everyone would memorize and live by that verse! Look at it again:

Proverbs 29:11 *A fool uttereth all his mind: but a wise man keepeth it in till afterwards.*

If there is anyone I know that has grown a lot and gotten a ton wiser over the last few years, it is my great friend Danny. But there was a time when he could not help but stick his foot in his mouth.

I remember riding with him in the church bus to school on Tuesday night. He turned off of Highway 74 onto Charles Road to pick up a friend that lived down in Shelby. As soon as he turned onto Charles Road, a police officer swooped in behind us and hit the blue lights. Danny went, "Oh no, I'm speeding!" He pulled over, the officer walked up and said, "Sir, do you know why I pulled you over?" Danny said, "Yes, sir, I was doing like fifty-five in a thirty-five!" The officer said, "No, I pulled you over because you ran that red light, but I appreciate your copping to speeding too!"

The officer went back to his car and I said, "Why didn't you tell him about the illegal immigrant you're smuggling in the trunk, and the drugs under the seat while you're at it!"

When an officer says, "Do you know why I pulled you over?" Your answer should be, "No, sir, I don't," because you may know something you were doing wrong, but he may not have actually pulled you over for that! You don't actually know why he pulled you over till he tells you! Sometimes, silence is golden!

Joseph really shouldn't have told his brothers his dream. Telling them the dream wasn't going to help make it come true and had no potential to do anything other than cause trouble.

Let me make a couple of applications here: first, learn now that many times silence is a wiser choice than speaking. Before you ever open your mouth, stop and consider the consequences of what you are about to say!

Before you tell your spouse how much you hated the meal, or how unhappy you are with the home he's provided, or how out-of-shape you think she is, or how dumb his kids are, stop and count the cost.

Before you ruin a friendship by saying something unkind, stop and count the cost.

Before you run headlong into the wrath of God by running down a church or the pastor, stop and count the cost.

Before you ruin your testimony by uttering a filthy word, stop and count the cost! Many times, silence is a wiser choice than speaking.

Second, beware of dream killers. I love people that aren't afraid to dream and dream big. Many years ago, there was a student at Yale University who wrote a paper describing his idea for a company that would ship packages all over the world, even doing it overnight. His learned professor was so impressed, that he gave the student a C on the paper, and told him the idea would never work. I don't know the professor's name. You don't know the professor's name. But every one of us know about Fred Smith, who went on to found a little company called Federal Express, now commonly known as FedEx. What if Fred Smith had given in to the dream killer?

Back when I was about thirteen a new preacher came to our church. The pastor I had grown up under worked with this little boy to make him a preacher. When the new preacher came in, my mom talked to him about me. For some reason, he had already evaluated me and made a decision. He told her, "He may be a lot of things in his life, but a preacher will never be one of them!"

Beware of dream killers!

Where is the next great medical breakthrough going to come from? Why not from you! Where is the next Billy Sunday? Maybe reading this book right now! Where is the next person who is going to found a huge, successful, Christ-honoring business? Why can't it be someone in my church or yours? Where is the next great missionary like David Livingston, who will shake an entire continent for God? Why shouldn't it be a boy who grows up here?

Listen to me, I don't know *what* God has called you to do, but I do know *how* He has called you to do it:

Ecclesiastes 9:10a *Whatsoever thy hand findeth to do, do it with thy might...*

Colossians 3:23 *And whatsoever ye do, do it heartily, as to the Lord, and not unto men;*

Dream big! Do big! From day one in the history of Cornerstone I've had a great, big dream for my church, and from day one I've tried very hard to avoid dream killers who would convince me that it can't be done.

Make a difference! Make a mark! Shoot for the moon, and if you miss, at least you'll go farther than people who only shoot for the tree-tops. Do something great with your life, all for the glory of God.

An Indignant Response
>**Genesis 37:8** *And his brethren said to him, Shalt thou indeed reign over us? or shalt thou indeed have dominion over us? And they hated him yet the more for his dreams, and for his words.*

The brothers of Joseph had one overriding belief; they were better than their little brother, and he would never, ever be in charge over them. But they were ignoring their own family history.

Abraham had two sons, Ishmael the older and Isaac the younger. God made Isaac the younger His choice instead of Ishmael the older. They liked that because they were descended from Grandpa Isaac.

Then Grandpa Isaac had two sons, Esau the older and Jacob the younger. But God chose Jacob the younger instead of Esau the older. They liked that, because Jacob was their daddy!

But now, when God is placing a special blessing on Joseph the younger, instead of any of them who were older, now all of the sudden they don't think it's right!

Isn't it amazing how people judge right or wrong based on whether or not something benefits them?

When the preacher preaches a hard message that lands on someone else, they say, "Way to go preacher; they needed that!" But when the next message lands on them, suddenly they don't like that kind of preaching.

When the officer pulls over the guy that came screaming past you a few miles back, you drive by and holler, "Throw the book at him; he's a menace to society!" But when the blue lights are behind you, you say, "C'mon man, it was only fifteen over; go catch a murderer or something instead of picking on me!"

When God allows a tragedy into someone else's life, you sit back in piety and say, "God is doing His will, trying to mold that person into His image." But when the tragedy is yours, you say, "God, I don't deserve this!"

People really do judge right or wrong based on whether or not something benefits them. There is a better way.

Psalm 115:3 *But our God is in the heavens: he hath done whatsoever he hath pleased.*

God chose to elevate Joseph, and his brothers could not stand it. Their indignant response was, "We'll never bow to you; we don't care what God says!" Be careful what you say for this very important reason:

Isaiah 55:8 *For my thoughts are not your thoughts, neither are your ways my ways, saith the LORD.* **9** *For as the heavens are higher than the earth, so are my ways higher than your ways, and my thoughts than your thoughts.*

Is it normal and customary for the elders to bow to the younger? No. But does God have the right to decree it that way if He so chooses? Certainly. He is in the heavens, He has done what He pleased, and He has the right to do as He pleases.

An Increased Vision

Genesis 37:9 *And he dreamed yet another dream, and told it his brethren,* **(after the last episode, you'd think that Joseph would have learned!)** *and said, Behold, I have dreamed a dream more; and, behold, the sun and the moon and the eleven stars made obeisance to me.* **10** *And he told it to his father, and to his brethren: and his father rebuked him, and said unto him, What is this dream that thou hast dreamed? Shall I and thy mother and thy brethren indeed come to bow down ourselves to thee to the earth?*

The last dream was easy enough to interpret. God was letting Joseph know that all eleven of his brothers were going to one day bow down to him. This dream was just as easy to understand, even though a couple of new things had been added. This time Joseph saw eleven stars bow to him. That was the exact same information as the last dream; it meant his brothers were going to bow down to him. But in this dream, Joseph also saw the sun and the moon bow to him. Everyone in the family clearly understood the implication; Joseph's mother and father would also bow down to him.

If you think it was unlikely and unheard of for older siblings to bow to a younger sibling, how much more unlikely was it for a mom and dad to bow to a child?

But get this, there is one more part of this that just adds to the incredulity. There is a part that had to make everybody but Joseph think he was a little nuts. His mother had already died! She died back in Genesis 35 while giving birth to Benjamin. She was not there in Egypt all those years later when the family came down and bowed to Joseph. Momma Rachel was bowing from the courts of Heaven, praising God for what He had done with her boy! This is just one more evidence that when you get to Heaven, you will still be aware of what happens here.

Have you ever felt like you were being watched, maybe even cheered on? You are:

Hebrews 12:1 *Wherefore seeing we also are compassed about with so great a cloud of witnesses, let us lay aside every weight, and the sin which doth so easily beset us, and let us run with patience the race that is set before us,*

That cloud of witnesses is the heroes of the faith from chapter eleven. Those who die in the Lord before we do, form a cheering gallery in the grandstand of Heaven, shouting my name, shouting your name, whispering to our hearts, "Come on, keep going, you can do it, don't stop, you're doing great, hang in there, I'm proud of you, keep at it!"

Praise God, not only is God cheering me on, but so is B.L. Queen, and godly old Mr. Landers, and Jerry Fite, and Mom Lookadoo. I think I'll just keep on going!

Who do you have cheering for you? Who is it that's waving your banner from the grandstands of glory? Those godly mothers, fathers, grandparents, spouses, and children that have preceded you in death. Listen with your spiritual ears, and you may well be able to hear them cheering you on!

An Individual Decision

Genesis 37:11 *And his brethren envied him; but his father observed the saying.*

Pay attention to this. There was one boy, one dream, one family, but two different responses to this episode. Joseph was related to all eleven brothers and to his father. The dream said that all of the brothers and the father would bow before him. There was no difference between what was being prophesied of Jacob and of the sons. But the sons envied, while the father observed. The only thing that was different was the reaction.

"Envied" we understand. But "observed" we may not. It means that Jacob stopped, took the information into his heart, carefully weighed it, and then treasured it up in his memory. In other words, after his initial negative response, he completely changed his reaction, and accepted what God had in store.

That sounds a great deal like another episode from Scripture. In Matthew 27 and Luke 23 we read about the crucifixion of Jesus. There were two thieves crucified with Him, one on either side. We are told that at the beginning of the crucifixion both of those thieves mocked and railed on Christ. But at some point in the proceedings, it dawned on one of them that the person being crucified beside him was not a mere man. That thief finally spoke up to the other thief and said, "Hush! Just hush! We deserve what we're getting, but this man has done nothing amiss!" Then he said, "Lord, remember me when thou comest into thy kingdom..."

Two people, equally close to salvation, one chose to accept the Son, one chose to reject Him. Ten older brothers, one father, equally close in proximity to Joseph, yet the brothers rejected the son and the father accepted him.

Everyone will make an individual, voluntary decision about what to do with Jesus, the Son of God. But there will come a point at which you will bow before Him, like it or not:

Philippians 2:9 *Wherefore God also hath highly exalted him, and given him a name which is above every name:* **10** *That at the name of Jesus every knee should bow, of things in heaven, and things in earth, and things under the earth;* **11** *And that every tongue should confess that Jesus Christ is Lord, to the glory of God the Father.*

Romans 14:11 *For it is written, As I live, saith the Lord, every knee shall bow to me, and every tongue shall confess to God.*

The brothers of Joseph chose to reject him, yet they still ended up having to bow before him. The father of Joseph chose to accept him, and he also ended up bowing before him. The outcome was the exact same; the only difference was that one bowed in joy and gratitude, the others bowed in terror. You are going to bow before Jesus one day, everyone is. My question is can you look forward to it?

Chapter 5
The Darkest Day

Genesis 37:12 *And his brethren went to feed their father's flock in Shechem.* **13** *And Israel said unto Joseph, Do not thy brethren feed the flock in Shechem? come, and I will send thee unto them. And he said to him, Here am I.* **14** *And he said to him, Go, I pray thee, see whether it be well with thy brethren, and well with the flocks; and bring me word again. So he sent him out of the vale of Hebron, and he came to Shechem.* **15** *And a certain man found him, and, behold, he was wandering in the field: and the man asked him, saying, What seekest thou?* **16** *And he said, I seek my brethren: tell me, I pray thee, where they feed their flocks.* **17** *And the man said, They are departed hence; for I heard them say, Let us go to Dothan. And Joseph went after his brethren, and found them in Dothan.* **18** *And when they saw him afar off, even before he came near unto them, they conspired against him to slay him.* **19** *And they said one to another, Behold, this dreamer cometh.* **20** *Come now therefore, and let us slay him, and cast him into some pit, and we will say, Some evil beast hath devoured him: and we shall see what will become of his dreams.* **21** *And Reuben heard it, and he delivered him out of their hands; and said, Let us not kill him.* **22** *And Reuben said unto them, Shed no blood, but cast him into this pit that is in the wilderness, and lay no hand upon him; that he might rid him out of their hands, to deliver him to his father again.* **23** *And it came to pass, when Joseph was come unto his brethren, that they stript Joseph out of his coat, his* *coat of many colours that was on him;* **24** *And they took him, and cast him into a pit: and the pit was empty, there was no water in it.* **25** *And they sat down to eat bread: and they lifted up their eyes and looked, and, behold, a company of Ishmeelites came from Gilead with their camels bearing spicery and balm and myrrh, going to carry it down to Egypt.* **26** *And Judah said unto his brethren, What profit is it if we slay our brother, and conceal his blood?* **27** *Come, and let us sell him to the Ishmeelites, and let not our hand be upon him; for he is our brother and our flesh. And his brethren were content.* **28** *Then there passed by Midianites merchantmen; and they drew and lifted up Joseph out of the pit, and sold Joseph to the Ishmeelites for twenty pieces of silver: and they brought Joseph into Egypt.* **29** *And Reuben returned unto the pit; and, behold, Joseph was not in the pit; and he rent his clothes.* **30** *And he returned unto his brethren, and said, The child is not; and I, whither shall I go?* **31** *And they took Joseph's coat, and killed a kid of the goats, and dipped the coat in the blood;* **32** *And they sent the coat of many colours, and they brought it to their father; and said, This have we found: know now whether it be thy son's coat or no.* **33** *And he knew it, and said, It is my son's coat; an evil beast hath devoured him; Joseph is without doubt rent in pieces.* **34** *And Jacob rent his clothes, and put sackcloth upon his loins, and mourned for his son many days.* **35** *And all his sons and all his daughters rose up to comfort him; but he refused to be comforted; and he said, For I will go down into the grave unto my son mourning. Thus his father wept for him.* **36** *And the Midianites sold him into Egypt unto Potiphar, an officer of Pharaoh's, and captain of the guard.*

On March 15, of A.D. 44, assassins attacked Julius Caesar. Caesar fought back like a wild man. But then, he noticed a familiar face among the attackers, Marcus Junius Brutus. Caesar not only trusted Brutus, he had regarded him as a son. When Caesar saw Brutus among the attackers, with his own dagger drawn, Caesar stopped struggling. He pulled the top part of his robe over his face, and asked, "You too, Brutus?" Caesar stopped struggling because life wasn't worth living if he was going to be betrayed by the ones he loved best.

There is no greater despair than being betrayed by those you love. Joseph could have related to that. No one, other than

Christ Himself, has ever experienced the depth of betrayal that Joseph did. And he went through it all at just seventeen years of age. There is no doubt that of all the dark days Joseph had in his lifetime, this was the worst, this was "The Darkest Day."

Joseph Sent on a Mission

Genesis 37:12 *And his brethren went to feed their father's flock in Shechem.* **13** *And Israel said unto Joseph, Do not thy brethren feed the flock in Shechem? come, and I will send thee unto them. And he said to him, Here am I.* **14** *And he said to him, Go, I pray thee, see whether it be well with thy brethren, and well with the flocks; and bring me word again. So he sent him out of the vale of Hebron, and he came to Shechem.*

It may have been the water of Shechem that led the boys to take their father's flock there. It was so well watered that it was perfect for large flocks of sheep, both in the water to drink and in all the vegetation to eat. I suspect there was another reason that led them there. They probably told their father the water was why they were going there, but Shechem was fifty miles away from their home base of Hebron. That is a good ways away from the oversight of the father. With the bad character these men had already demonstrated, they definitely would have liked that part of it.

So when Jacob sent Joseph out to check on his brothers, it was no easy task. Dad was asking his seventeen year old son to go fifty miles, most likely on foot, to fulfill this mission.

This says something about how trustworthy Joseph was! How many seventeen year olds can you trust to go on a hundred mile round trip, with no supervision, and do a good job, with no playing around along the way? Come to think of it, these days, how many twenty-seven year olds or thirty-seven year olds could you trust like that?

So he sent him out of the vale of Hebron, and he came to Shechem.

Genesis 37:15 *And a certain man found him, and, behold, he was wandering in the field: and the man asked him, saying, What seekest thou?* **16** *And he said, I seek my brethren: tell me, I pray thee, where they feed their flocks.*

When Joseph got to Shechem, where his brothers were supposed to be, they weren't there. Only one ignorant of their poor character would be surprised at that.

A man found Joseph wandering the fields looking for them, and asked him what he was looking for. Joseph said, "I'm looking for my brothers, can you tell me where they're feeding the flock?" It turns out that he could:

Genesis 37:17 *And the man said, They are departed hence; for I heard them say, Let us go to Dothan. And Joseph went after his brethren, and found them in Dothan.*

Now please understand that, as well watered as Shechem was, there really was no good reason for these guys to pull out and go to Dothan. Dothan was twelve to fifteen miles north of Shechem. Shechem was where they told their dad they would be, but Dothan is where they ended up. Again, they seemed to like not being accountable, they seemed to like doing their own thing. I am guessing that they figured if Dad did send Joseph to check on them, he would never find them in Dothan. But trust me, if you open your mouth, somebody will overhear, and the word will get out.

Joseph Spotted by His Brothers

Genesis 37:18 *And when they saw him afar off, even before he came near unto them, they conspired against him to slay him.*

Let me see if you have your brain in gear at this point. How did Joseph's brothers recognize him from such a long way off? His coat of many colors! I know Jacob meant well giving that coat to Joseph, but he may as well have put a "kick me" sign on his back.

Before Joseph ever got near them, they were already planning to kill him.

Genesis 37:19 *And they said one to another, Behold, this dreamer cometh.*

There are different ways in Hebrew to say "dreamer." The way they chose to say it was dripping with sarcasm. It basically means "the master of dreams!"

Isn't it interesting that this is the only thing they could see in him? You know there was much more to Joseph than just his dreams, but his brothers chose to see only the one thing that they hated most about him.

But isn't that the way it is even today? When somebody doesn't like a brother or sister in Christ, they will never focus on the good things about them; all they will think of is the one or two things they despise about them. This is true when a marriage is experiencing difficulties; it is true when teenagers get ill with each other; it is true when preachers fuss and fight. May I give you some good, Biblical advice? If you are at odds with a brother or sister in Christ, don't just focus on the one bad thing; remember that there are probably quite a few good things about them as well!

Genesis 37:20 *Come now therefore, and let us slay him, and cast him into some pit, and we will say, Some evil beast hath devoured him: and we shall see what will become of his dreams.*

It was all about the dreams that God gave Joseph. They hated what God was going to do with Joseph, so they determined to kill him, hide the body, and concoct a story about an animal killing him. This was their own brother! How seared does your conscience have to be to sit around and come up with this like it is no big deal? There are simply no depths to which sin cannot take you.

Genesis 37:21 *And Reuben heard it, and he delivered him out of their hands; and said, Let us not kill him.* **22** *And Reuben said unto them, Shed no blood, but cast him into this pit that is in the wilderness, and lay no hand upon him; that he might rid him out of their hands, to deliver him to his father again.*

Reuben heard it. That lets us know that he isn't the one that said it. And that, along with the fact that he objected to it, is interesting for this reason: Reuben was the firstborn. Most of the blessings that the father was giving to Joseph would normally have gone to Reuben. If there is anyone that stood to gain from the death of Joseph, it was Reuben. To me, this doesn't tell me anything good about Reuben, it tells me something good about God. God is able to raise up help for you from the most unlikely of sources. We tend to sell God short. We figure He can only raise up help for us through people close to us. God is God, He can make the worst of our enemies reach out and help us if He so desires! Next time one of your enemies helps you, just remember that God is still God.

Joseph Scared and Helpless
Genesis 37:23 *And it came to pass, when Joseph was come unto his brethren, that they stript Joseph out of his coat, his coat of many colours that was on him;* **24** *And they took him, and cast him into a pit: and the pit was empty, there was no water in it.* **25a** *And they sat down to eat bread:*

There is no way to overstate just how awful and dark this moment was for Joseph. Joseph came to his brothers, not suspecting a thing, and at a given signal, all of them jumped him. Ten against one, the boy had no chance. They ripped his robe off of him; twenty angry hands grabbing and tearing and clawing at him. They threw him down into a pit, a dry, cold, lifeless hole in the ground. What must it have been like to find yourself falling, wondering how far it will be till you hit bottom. You have to wonder how bruised and battered he was from hitting the ground. Did he break or fracture any bones when he hit? Did he bust his nose by hitting face first into the ground? There is no good way to land when you're thrown into a pit like a piece of garbage.

When Joseph caught his breath, brushed the dirt out of his eyes, and got adjusted to the darkness around him, he saw that the pit was empty. There was no food, no water, and no way out. And what did his brothers do? They sat down, right there at the pit, and had lunch.

Years later, the brothers themselves said something about this moment that will just break your heart:

Genesis 42:21 *And they said one to another, We are verily guilty concerning our brother, in that we saw the anguish of his soul, when he besought us, and we would not hear.*

While they were up there eating their meal, Joseph was down below them in that pit, hurting, crying like a baby, begging them to please get him out, please don't kill him, please don't leave him there. His brothers, these were his brothers that were doing this.

Joseph Sold into Slavery

Genesis 37:25b... *and they lifted up their eyes and looked, and, behold, a company of Ishmeelites came from Gilead with their camels bearing spicery and balm and myrrh, going to carry it down to Egypt.* **26** *And Judah said unto his brethren, What profit is it if we slay our brother, and conceal his blood?* **27** *Come, and let us sell him to the Ishmeelites, and let not our hand be upon him; for he is our brother and our flesh. And his brethren were content.*

While Joseph's brothers were sitting there with crumbs in their beards, Joseph down below them begging for mercy, they looked up and saw a caravan. Verse 25 lets us know that there were Ishmeelites in the caravan, verse 28 tells us that there were Midianites as well. That caravan was heading down into Egypt to sell their merchandise.

That gave Joseph's brothers an idea, and according to verse 26, their idea was motivated by the potential for profit. They decided that instead of killing Joseph, which would make them feel good but not gain them anything, they would sell him into slavery instead. God used their greed to save Joseph's life.

Genesis 37:28 *Then there passed by Midianites merchantmen; and they drew and lifted up Joseph out of the pit, and sold Joseph to the Ishmeelites for twenty pieces of silver: and they brought Joseph into Egypt.*

Genesis 37:36 *And the Midianites sold him into Egypt unto Potiphar, an officer of Pharaoh's, and captain of the guard.*

When Joseph got up that morning, he was in familiar territory, a beloved child of the father. When he saw the sun go down that night, he was heading into a strange land, arms and legs in shackles, a seventeen year old slave.

Joseph Separated from the Father

Genesis 37:29 *And Reuben returned unto the pit; and, behold, Joseph was not in the pit; and he rent his clothes.* **30** *And he returned unto his brethren, and said, The child is not; and I, whither shall I go?*

This gives us another important detail in this episode. After they threw Joseph into the pit, Reuben went off somewhere. Maybe it was to tend to the flock, who knows. But whatever the reason, when his little brother needed him most, he was somewhere else. There could not have been anything in the universe more important than saving his brother's life. Reuben came back to the pit, Joseph was already long gone, and the other brothers were splitting the money they got from selling him. Two lousy pieces of silver per brother! I have to guess that when Reuben tore his own clothes in anguish, maybe, just maybe it began to dawn on them what they had done.

For Reuben, this was devastating. As the oldest, his father was going to hold him responsible. You can hear that in his voice when he said, "The child is not; and I, whither shall I go?"

Genesis 37:31 *And they took Joseph's coat, and killed a kid of the goats, and dipped the coat in the blood;* **32** *And they sent the coat of many colours, and they brought it to their father; and said, This have we found: know now whether it be thy son's coat or no.*

Did you notice that they were so careful not to lie and say that Joseph had been killed? They just made sure their father would assume it. "We wouldn't want to actually lie or anything. Sell our brother into slavery, no big deal, but we sure wouldn't want to lie, now would we." It is amazing how we comfort ourselves with small righteousnesses in the midst of enormous transgressions.

Genesis 37:33 *And he knew it, and said, It is my son's coat; an evil beast hath devoured him; Joseph is without doubt rent in pieces.* **34** *And Jacob rent his clothes, and put sackcloth upon his loins, and mourned for his son many days.*

These boys, just like most sinners, were as dumb as dirt. They somehow thought that their father would get over it, and love them like he loved Joseph since Joseph wasn't there anymore. They couldn't seem to grasp that their father's life was wrapped up in Joseph and that he was never going to be the same.

Genesis 37:35 *And all his sons and all his daughters rose up to comfort him; but he refused to be comforted; and he said, For I will go down into the grave unto my son mourning. Thus his father wept for him.*

When this verse says that his sons tried to comfort him, does anything very obvious occur to you? ***If they really wanted***

to comfort him, all they had to do was tell him where Joseph was, and go buy him back! But they weren't going to do that, because they thought more of themselves than they did their father, and they thought more of themselves than they did of Joseph. They could have ended this at any time, and they chose not to. This was absolutely Joseph's, and Jacob's, darkest day.

May I make a few applications at the close of this chapter?

First, our dark days are not really very dark when compared with what Joseph went through. We really tend to make little things out to be very big.

Second, God used something awful to save Joseph from something even worse. What could be worse than being sold into slavery? How about being murdered right there on the spot! God sent those Midianite/Ishmaelites by at just the right time. Joseph recovered from being sold into slavery, but no one ever recovers from being dead!

Third, the pit prepared Joseph for the rest of the hard times in his life. How well do you think Joseph would have handled Potiphar's house or the prison without the preparation of the pit? The spiritual strength many of you now have would not have come without the trials that God allowed you to go through. The trials that many of you are now going through are going to give you the spiritual strength you need for the trials yet to come.

Fourth, Joseph did not know why he was going through this trial, but he knew the God of the why, and that was enough for him.

Fifth, the darkest day of Joseph led to the brightest days of Joseph, and the same thing will be true for us if we stay faithful like Joseph did.

Dear Lord, Shepherd us through our darkest days!

Chapter 6
What His Brothers Could Not Take

Genesis 39:1 *And Joseph was brought down to Egypt; and Potiphar, an officer of Pharaoh, captain of the guard, an Egyptian, bought him of the hands of the Ishmeelites, which had brought him down thither.* **2** *And the LORD was with Joseph, and he was a prosperous man; and he was in the house of his master the Egyptian.* **3** *And his master saw that the LORD was with him, and that the LORD made all that he did to prosper in his hand.* **4** *And Joseph found grace in his sight, and he served him: and he made him overseer over his house, and all that he had he put into his hand.* **5** *And it came to pass from the time that he had made him overseer in his house, and over all that he had, that the LORD blessed the Egyptian's house for Joseph's sake; and the blessing of the LORD was upon all that he had in the house, and in the field.* **6** *And he left all that he had in Joseph's hand; and he knew not ought he had, save the bread which he did eat. And Joseph was a goodly person, and well favoured.* **7** *And it came to pass after these things, that his master's wife cast her eyes upon Joseph; and she said, Lie with me.* **8** *But he refused, and said unto his master's wife, Behold, my master wotteth not what is with me in the house, and he hath committed all that he hath to my hand;* **9** *There is none greater in this house than I; neither hath he kept back any thing from me but thee, because thou art his wife: how then can I do this great wickedness, and sin against God?* **10** *And it came to pass, as she spake to Joseph day by day, that he hearkened not unto* *her, to lie by her, or to be with her.* **11** *And it came to pass about this time, that Joseph went into the house to do his business; and there was none of the men of the house there within.* **12** *And she caught him by his garment, saying, Lie with me: and he left his garment in her hand, and fled, and got him out.* **13** *And it came to pass, when she saw that he had left his garment in her hand, and was fled forth,* **14** *That she called unto the men of her house, and spake unto them, saying, See, he hath brought in an Hebrew unto us to mock us; he came in unto me to lie with me, and I cried with a loud voice:* **15** *And it came to pass, when he heard that I lifted up my voice and cried, that he left his garment with me, and fled, and got him out.* **16** *And she laid up his garment by her, until his lord came home.* **17** *And she spake unto him according to these words, saying, The Hebrew servant, which thou hast brought unto us, came in unto me to mock me:* **18** *And it came to pass, as I lifted up my voice and cried, that he left his garment with me, and fled out.* **19** *And it came to pass, when his master heard the words of his wife, which she spake unto him, saying, After this manner did thy servant to me; that his wrath was kindled.* **20** *And Joseph's master took him, and put him into the prison, a place where the king's prisoners were bound: and he was there in the prison.* **21** *But the LORD was with Joseph, and shewed him mercy, and gave him favour in the sight of the keeper of the prison.* **22** *And the keeper of the prison committed to Joseph's hand all the prisoners that were in the prison; and whatsoever they did there, he was the doer of it.* **23** *The keeper of the prison looked not to any thing that was under his hand; because the LORD was with him, and that which he did, the LORD made it to prosper.*

    On Joseph's darkest day, his brothers took all they possibly could take from him. They took his precious robe... they took his family... they took his freedom... but there is one thing they could not take from him. It is something that a person can give up, but no one can take it away. That something is *character*, what the Bible calls "integrity."

    Before we examine the character of Joseph, let's look at the over-riding care of the Lord.

The Care of the Lord
Genesis 39:1 *And Joseph was brought down to Egypt; and Potiphar, an officer of Pharaoh, captain of the guard, an Egyptian, bought him of the hands of the Ishmeelites, which had brought him down thither.*

The hand of God is so very, very exact. Joseph could have ended up being bought by any one of hundreds of thousands of people in Egypt.

He could have been bought by Achmed, the camel dung dealer...

He could have been bought by Swahib, the cucumber picker...

But in the mercy, the providence, the care of God, Joseph was bought by Potiphar, the very captain of Pharaoh's guard. This was the beginning of Joseph's journey to the throne, being purchased by one so well connected as Potiphar.

Genesis 39:2 *And the LORD was with Joseph, and he was a prosperous man; and he was in the house of his master the Egyptian.*

Notice those words "in the house." They are very important. Most slaves were not in the house, most slaves were out in the open fields, treated no better than cattle under the rod. Most slaves had short life spans; their cruel treatment tended to send them to an early grave. But God, in His care, made sure that not only was Joseph bought by Potiphar, he was made to live and serve in the house of Potiphar.

The Character of Joseph
There are some remarkable things to notice about the character of Joseph. First of all, Joseph kept his character when he lost his standing.

Genesis 39:3 *And his master saw that the LORD was with him, and that the LORD made all that he did to prosper in his hand.* **4** *And Joseph found grace in his sight, and he served him: and he made him overseer over his house, and all that he had he put into his hand.* **5** *And it came to pass from the time that he had made him overseer in his house, and over all that he had, that the LORD blessed the Egyptian's house for Joseph's sake; and the blessing of the LORD was upon all that he had in the house, and in the field.*

Joseph, at home, was the favored son. In Egypt, he found himself a servant in the house of a heathen. There are few things that chafe a person worse than being deprived of their standing unjustly. Think of a young person who should have been valedictorian, but somehow saw that honor unfairly go to another...

Think of a person who was due a promotion at work, and was instead demoted...

Think of a person who has given thirty years of service to a company, and then been forced to retire so that company could hire a younger worker...

When such a thing occurs, a person's nature demands that they strike back in anger and assert their rights. It takes a person of very rare quality to maintain his godly attitude and testimony when he has been deprived of his standing. But that very thing is what Christ voluntarily did and instructed us to do as well.

Philippians 2:5 *Let this mind be in you, which was also in Christ Jesus:* **6** *Who, being in the form of God, thought it not robbery to be equal with God:* **7** *But made himself of no reputation, and took upon him the form of a servant, and was made in the likeness of men:* **8** *And being found in fashion as a man, he humbled himself, and became obedient unto death, even the death of the cross.*

Our standing here, now, is truly of very little consequence. We must maintain our character in the face of deprived standing because our standing as children of the King can never be taken away! Joseph was a servant in a heathen's house, but he never for a moment ceased to be the son of his father.

We also see that Joseph kept his character when there was no one to notice if he lost it.

Genesis 39:6a *And he left all that he had in Joseph's hand; and he knew not ought he had, save the bread which he did eat.*

Joseph is to be admired now, for he was clearly admired then by the people who were nearest to him and knew him best. Potiphar thought so much of him he did not even bother to check behind him or watch to make sure that he behaved. How many people can be trusted to that degree? It is easy to maintain one's character when you are being watched day and night. But to know that no one is watching, to know that no one will check behind you, and yet still maintain your character, that is of inestimable worth!

Joseph also kept his character even when he became attractive.

Genesis 39:6b *...And Joseph was a goodly person, and well favoured.*

Far be it from me or anyone else to sound unkind, but in many areas, an unattractive person has an easier time maintaining good character than an attractive person does. If a guy is so ugly that people spray Roundup on the mistletoe before inviting him to a Christmas party, he will probably have an easy time maintaining his purity. If a girl lays on the beach during high tide and finds that even the tide won't take her out, she will probably have an easy time maintaining her purity.

But these things were not true of Joseph! Joseph was an attractive, well-built young man, yet he refused to allow his looks to compromise his character.

Having achieved the feat of living to the ripe, old age of forty, I have had the privilege of seeing a "time lapse truth." I have been able to watch as (forgive me all you to whom this applies) relatively unattractive kids stay on fire for God, and maintain their godly character. And I have then seen that some of them, as they grow up, are transformed from ugly duckling to beautiful swan. Unfortunately, some of them also have their character transformed from that of angel to devil!

For you that are less than perfect, but fully on fire for God, I have this hope. May you never get attractive enough to compromise your character! Joseph kept his character even when he became attractive.

Joseph also kept his character when it would have felt good to give up his character.

Genesis 39:7 *And it came to pass after these things, that his master's wife cast her eyes upon Joseph; and she said, Lie with me.* **8** *But he refused, and said unto his master's wife, Behold, my master wotteth not what is with me in the house, and he hath committed all that he hath to my hand;* **9** *There is none greater in this house than I; neither hath he kept back any thing* *from me but thee, because thou art his wife: how then can I do this great wickedness, and sin against God?*

Anyone who tells a person that sin is no fun is either lying or deranged, perhaps both. The Bible gives testimony to what we already know. At least for a while, sin is enjoyable.

Hebrews 11:25 *Choosing rather to suffer affliction with the people of God, than to enjoy the pleasures of sin for a season;*

It felt good for David to sin with Bathsheba. It felt good for Judas to take the thirty pieces of silver. It felt good for Lucifer to imagine being like the most high. It felt good for Eve to put the fruit to her lips. Sin is only pleasurable for a season, but it is pleasurable!

Every person faces the temptation to sin in ways that would be pleasurable. Whether the temptation is to fornicate or get revenge or lust or greed, the godly person must retain his character when it would be pleasurable to forsake it.

A well known preacher, who operated a girl's home known nationally, recently departed into sin. Faced with the temptation to fulfill the lusts of his flesh, he threw away his ministry, his reputation, his wife, his kids, and his grand kids, for a little trollop young enough to be his daughter. He was faced with a pleasurable temptation, and he abandoned his character for it. The damage will never be undone. He did more harm in a moment than any amount of good he did in twenty years of ministry.

Joseph was different. Joseph kept his character even when it would have felt good to give up his character.

We also see that Joseph kept his character when he faced temptation every single day.

Genesis 39:10 *And it came to pass, as she spake to Joseph day by day, that he hearkened not unto her, to lie by her, or to be with her.*

I admire the fact that he would not even get near her! John Wesley said, "Those that would be kept from harm must keep themselves out of harm's way." That is utterly Biblical:

Romans 13:14 *But put ye on the Lord Jesus Christ, and make not provision for the flesh, to fulfil the lusts thereof.*

No one ever sinned without giving themselves a chance to do so! Joseph, though, was faced with a temptation that was not sporadic. There was no way that he could simply stay out of the house; he was a servant of Potiphar. He refused all of her advances, he would not be near her or lie by her, but he, nonetheless, was faced with her temptation every single day. A temptation for a moment is easily withstood, but a temptation faced every single day is much more difficult to withstand. But a key to Joseph maintaining his character is perhaps seen in what Scripture *does not* say. At no time does Scripture indicate that Joseph used the duration of the temptation as a justification to give in!

Here is a wonderful wealth-building plan for a pastor: simply find someone to agree to give you a dollar for every time you hear someone say, "But preacher, a person can only take so much!" What is that? That is a rationalization that if a temptation goes on consistently for a long time it must be acceptable to give in. God forbid! No amount of daily temptation is ever a valid justification for abandoning our character.

Joseph also kept his character when he knew he was going to lose everything else.

Genesis 39:11 *And it came to pass about this time, that Joseph went into the house to do his business; and there was none of the men of the house there within.* **12** *And she caught him by his garment, saying, Lie with me: and he left his garment in her hand, and fled, and got him out.* **13** *And it came to pass, when she saw that he had left his garment in her hand, and was fled forth,* **14** *That she called unto the men of her house, and spake unto them, saying, See, he hath brought in an Hebrew unto us to mock us; he came in unto me to lie with me, and I cried with a loud voice:* **15** *And it came to pass, when he heard that I lifted up my voice and cried, that he left his garment with me, and fled, and got him out.* **16** *And she laid up his garment by her, until his lord came home.* **17** *And she spake unto him according to these words, saying, The Hebrew servant, which thou hast brought unto us, came in unto me to mock me:* **18** *And it came to pass, as I lifted up my voice and cried, that he left his garment with me, and fled out.* **19** *And it came to pass, when his master heard the words of his wife, which she spake unto him, saying, After this manner did thy servant to me; that his wrath was kindled.*

It would be easy to read this and conclude that Joseph wasted his time and effort. He kept his character and look what happened to him! Exactly. Look at what happened to him. Look at the next verse.

Genesis 39:20 *And Joseph's master took him, and put him into the prison, a place where the king's prisoners were bound: and he was there in the prison.*

Hallelujah! Amen! Glory! And no, I'm not crazy. (And as I write these words, my wife lies beside me in bed, laughing hysterically, knowing that a great number of people disagree. Thanks, Honey). Yes, I know I'm shouting in my writing over the fact that Joseph ended up in prison. There is a really good reason for that. In Egypt, the captain of Pharaoh's guard was the chief executioner! So now you can say it with me! Glory! Hallelujah! It is an absolute miracle, one more time, that Joseph didn't end up dead! This is the second time he has been on the verge of death and had God deliver him. General population isn't near as bad as death row. Look what happened next.

Genesis 39:21 *But the LORD was with Joseph, and shewed him mercy, and gave him favour in the sight of the keeper of the prison.* **22** *And the keeper of the prison committed to Joseph's hand all the prisoners that were in the prison; and whatsoever they did there, he was the doer of it.* **23** *The keeper of the prison looked not to any thing that was under his hand; because the LORD was with him, and that which he did, the LORD made it to prosper.*

I don't think we have many young people with Joseph's kind of character. You say, "Preacher, don't chase anybody away!" I'm not trying to chase anybody away, but I'm a lot more concerned about my young people than I am of most anything else. If we build a big new building and have some of my church kids die and go to hell, I'm a failure. If we build a big new building and have these kids turn out like reprobate heathens while sitting on these pews, I'm a failure. I am weary of young people fornicating and drinking and sneaking around and listening to wicked music and getting tattoos and body piercings and talking like gang-bangers and lying and gossiping and being snotty. I want some godly, sold out, committed young people; young people like Joseph, who won't give up their character for anything in this world. Most everything else can be *taken from you*, but *your character can only be given away by you.*

Chapter 7
The Puzzle Table

Genesis 40:1 *And it came to pass after these things, that the butler of the king of Egypt and his baker had offended their lord the king of Egypt.* **2** *And Pharaoh was wroth against two of his officers, against the chief of the butlers, and against the chief of the bakers.* **3** *And he put them in ward in the house of the captain of the guard, into the prison, the place where Joseph was bound.* **4** *And the captain of the guard charged Joseph with them, and he served them: and they continued a season in ward.* **5** *And they dreamed a dream both of them, each man his dream in one night, each man according to the interpretation of his dream, the butler and the baker of the king of Egypt, which were bound in the prison.* **6** *And Joseph came in unto them in the morning, and looked upon them, and, behold, they were sad.* **7** *And he asked Pharaoh's officers that were with him in the ward of his lord's house, saying, Wherefore look ye so sadly to day?* **8** *And they said unto him, We have dreamed a dream, and there is no interpreter of it. And Joseph said unto them, Do not interpretations belong to God? tell me them, I pray you.* **9** *And the chief butler told his dream to Joseph, and said to him, In my dream, behold, a vine was before me;* **10** *And in the vine were three branches: and it was as though it budded, and her blossoms shot forth; and the clusters thereof brought forth ripe grapes:* **11** *And Pharaoh's cup was in my hand: and I took the grapes, and pressed them into Pharaoh's cup, and I gave the cup into Pharaoh's hand.* **12** *And Joseph said unto him,*

This is the interpretation of it: The three branches are three days: **13** *Yet within three days shall Pharaoh lift up thine head, and restore thee unto thy place: and thou shalt deliver Pharaoh's cup into his hand, after the former manner when thou wast his butler.* **14** *But think on me when it shall be well with thee, and shew kindness, I pray thee, unto me, and make mention of me unto Pharaoh, and bring me out of this house:* **15** *For indeed I was stolen away out of the land of the Hebrews: and here also have I done nothing that they should put me into the dungeon.* **16** *When the chief baker saw that the interpretation was good, he said unto Joseph, I also was in my dream, and, behold, I had three white baskets on my head:* **17** *And in the uppermost basket there was of all manner of bakemeats for Pharaoh; and the birds did eat them out of the basket upon my head.* **18** *And Joseph answered and said, This is the interpretation thereof: The three baskets are three days:* **19** *Yet within three days shall Pharaoh lift up thy head from off thee, and shall hang thee on a tree; and the birds shall eat thy flesh from off thee.* **20** *And it came to pass the third day, which was Pharaoh's birthday, that he made a feast unto all his servants: and he lifted up the head of the chief butler and of the chief baker among his servants.* **21** *And he restored the chief butler unto his butlership again; and he gave the cup into Pharaoh's hand:* **22** *But he hanged the chief baker: as Joseph had interpreted to them.* **23** *Yet did not the chief butler remember Joseph, but forgat him.*

In many homes, you will find a "puzzle person." Where you find puzzle people, you will find a puzzle table. It is usually in some out of the way place, where the puzzle person can take plenty of uninterrupted time to put all of the pieces together just right. In this text, you will observe God, the greatest of all puzzle people, setting up a table in an Egyptian prison and taking a few years to put the puzzle of Joseph's life together. So let's head back to that prison and look at another episode from the life of Joseph.

The Moving of God
   Genesis 40:1 *And it came to pass after these things, that the butler of the king of Egypt and his baker had offended their lord the king of Egypt.*

Notice the timing. After these things, after Potiphar's wife, after Joseph ended up in prison. Remember that...

The butler and baker of a king were two of the most important men in the kingdom. Everything the king ate or drank had to come through them; they were personally responsible for making sure he did not get poisoned. They were so important that they were usually members of the royal family!

If they ended up in prison, it is a good indication that the king suspected one or both of them of trying to kill him. Again, all of this happened after the episode in Potiphar's house.

Genesis 40:1 *And it came to pass after these things, that the butler of the king of Egypt and his baker had offended their lord the king of Egypt.* **2** *And Pharaoh was wroth against two of his officers, against the chief of the butlers, and against the chief of the bakers.* **3** *And he put them in ward in the house of the captain of the guard, into the prison, the place where Joseph was bound.*

God is perfect in timing and placement. If they had offended the king earlier... or later... they would not have come into contact with Joseph. If they had been killed instantly, as the king usually did in cases like this, they would not have come into contact with Joseph. If they had been placed somewhere else, they would not have come into contact with Joseph. Never forget, God is perfect in all of His ways!

The Ministry of Joseph

Genesis 40:4 *And the captain of the guard charged Joseph with them, and he served them: and they continued a season in ward.*

Joseph was still a Hebrew slave even though he was in charge of the prison. He was expected to serve these important prisoners. By now, he could have gotten bitter and decided to do as little as possible, but that was just not in the character of Joseph.

Genesis 40:5 *And they dreamed a dream both of them, each man his dream in one night, each man according to the interpretation of his dream, the butler and the baker of the king of Egypt, which were bound in the prison.*

Two men had dreams, dreams that they could not understand. And what did Joseph have great experience in? Oh how great are the workings of God! How many years ago in that field did all of this start?! What must Joseph have thought? His dreams got him into this!

And both of them dreaming like this in one night? Oh, see the hand of our God at work!

Genesis 40:6 *And Joseph came in unto them in the morning, and looked upon them, and, behold, they were sad.* **7** *And he asked Pharaoh's officers that were with him in the ward of his lord's house, saying, Wherefore look ye so sadly to day?*

Joseph actually cared. Joseph actually cared! A Hebrew boy, the favored son of his father, stripped of everything that he loved and valued, sold as a captive to heathens in a foreign land, lied about by a wicked woman, imprisoned unjustly, still cared for others. The only way that this is possible is for a person to *choose* to care for others. It is easy to care when things are well. To care when things are not well, and to care for the race of people who are responsible for a great deal of your trouble, that takes character. Joseph did just that, caring for two Egyptians, when he himself was a slave in an Egyptian prison.

Genesis 40:8 *And they said unto him, We have dreamed a dream, and there is no interpreter of it. And Joseph said unto them, Do not interpretations belong to God? tell me them, I pray you.*

All of Joseph's troubles started with a dream and here he is still serving in the midst of more dreams. Of what value is a servant's heart like this? I have yet to see the first real servant with the right focus that was miserable.

The Meaning of the Dreams

Genesis 40:9 *And the chief butler told his dream to Joseph, and said to him, In my dream, behold, a vine was before me;* **10** *And in the vine were three branches: and it was as though it budded, and her blossoms shot forth; and the clusters thereof brought forth ripe grapes:* **11** *And Pharaoh's cup was in my hand: and I took the grapes, and pressed them into Pharaoh's cup, and I gave the cup into Pharaoh's hand.* **12** *And Joseph said unto him, This is the interpretation of it: The three* *branches are three days:* **13** *Yet within three days shall Pharaoh lift up thine head, and restore thee unto thy place: and thou shalt deliver Pharaoh's cup into his hand, after the former manner when thou wast his butler.* **14** *But think on me when it shall be well with thee, and shew kindness, I pray thee, unto me, and make mention of me unto Pharaoh, and bring me out of this house:* **15** *For indeed I was stolen away out of the land of the Hebrews: and here also have I done nothing that they should put me into the dungeon.* **16** *When the chief baker saw that the interpretation was good, he said unto Joseph, I also was in my dream, and, behold, I had three white baskets on my head:* **17** *And in the uppermost basket there was of all manner of bakemeats for Pharaoh; and the birds did eat them out of the basket upon my head.* **18** *And Joseph answered and said, This is the interpretation thereof: The three baskets are three days:* **19** *Yet within three days shall Pharaoh lift up thy head from off thee, and shall hang thee on a tree; and the birds shall eat thy flesh from off thee.*

    A very noticeable, admirable trait of Joseph was his consistency. Not too long past he had been one hundred percent honest in his interpretation of a dream that would be regarded negatively by others. He now finds himself in a position where one of the two dreams will have a very negative interpretation, yet he gives it honestly anyway.

    To the butler Joseph was able to give good news. "Your dream of the vine with the three branches means that in three days Pharaoh will release you from this prison and restore you to your former position." To the baker Joseph was not able to give good news. "The three baskets on your head with the birds eating out of them mean that in three days Pharaoh is going to take your head off of your body and hang your body on a tree for the birds to eat."

    Joseph, in this, becomes an excellent pattern for men of God to follow. If we are true with Scripture and the way we apply it to people's lives, we will not always be able to give a positive message. People in sin need to be scalded, not soothed. People need to hear of Heaven but also of Hell. People need to be encouraged with the rewards that Christ is bringing with Him when He comes, but they also need to understand the law of sowing and reaping. It is a poor excuse for a man of God that will say something positive to a person who is in desperate need of hearing the negative!

The Molding of Joseph

Genesis 40:20 *And it came to pass the third day, which was Pharaoh's birthday, that he made a feast unto all his servants: and he lifted up the head of the chief butler and of the chief baker among his servants.* **21** *And he restored the chief butler unto his butlership again; and he gave the cup into Pharaoh's hand:* **22** *But he hanged the chief baker: as Joseph had interpreted to them.* **23** *Yet did not the chief butler remember Joseph, but forgat him.*

Every trial will mold you but the way it molds you will be determined by how you respond to it. Joseph was once again betrayed by someone who should have loved him. Joseph took time to minister to and care for the chief butler. But when the chief butler was released from prison he "forgot" about Joseph. One does not forget about a man like that by accident! This was not a slip of the mind; it was a choice of the will. He calculated that Pharaoh had been mad at him once before, had just now released him, and he did not want to do anything to rock the boat. So Joseph was forgotten, intentionally, by a man who owed him dearly.

Joseph at that point had a choice to make. Respond in bitterness or refuse to become bitter. In all of Joseph's life, he is remarkable for the fact that no hint of bitterness is ever recorded! Joseph allowed this latest agonizing disappointment to mold him positively rather than negatively. How do we know this? A bitter man will, oh so quickly, "cut off his nose to spite his face." The chief butler, two full years later, saw an opportunity to endear himself to Pharaoh by using Joseph. Pharaoh dreamed a dream and needed an interpreter. So, not to get too far ahead of ourselves, the man "conveniently remembered" Joseph and his uncanny ability. Pharaoh summoned Joseph, who then had a choice to make. Interpret Pharaoh's dream, with no promise of any reward of any kind, and hope for the best. Or he could do something that would, most definitely have the promise of reward. Joseph could have looked dumbfounded before Pharaoh, and pretended not to know a thing about interpreting dreams! He would doubtless have been sent back to prison, at the very least. But the butler would most assuredly have been killed!

    Thankfully for both of them, and later for the whole world, Joseph had allowed his terrible disappointment in prison mold him into a better man, rather than a bitter one. And thus, the hand of God picked up the puzzle pieces of Joseph's life, snapped the last few pieces into place, and produced a man fit for the palace from the wreckage of a man who had been in the prison.

Chapter 8
The Turning of the Tide

Genesis 41:1 *And it came to pass at the end of two full years, that Pharaoh dreamed: and, behold, he stood by the river.* **2** *And, behold, there came up out of the river seven well favoured kine and fatfleshed; and they fed in a meadow.* **3** *And, behold, seven other kine came up after them out of the river, ill favoured and leanfleshed; and stood by the other kine upon the brink of the river.* **4** *And the ill favoured and leanfleshed kine did eat up the seven well favoured and fat kine. So Pharaoh awoke.* **5** *And he slept and dreamed the second time: and, behold, seven ears of corn came up upon one stalk, rank and good.* **6** *And, behold, seven thin ears and blasted with the east wind sprung up after them.* **7** *And the seven thin ears devoured the seven rank and full ears. And Pharaoh awoke, and, behold, it was a dream.* **8** *And it came to pass in the morning that his spirit was troubled; and he sent and called for all the magicians of Egypt, and all the wise men thereof: and Pharaoh told them his dream; but there was none that could interpret them unto Pharaoh.* **9** *Then spake the chief butler unto Pharaoh, saying, I do remember my faults this day:* **10** *Pharaoh was wroth with his servants, and put me in ward in the captain of the guard's house, both me and the chief baker:* **11** *And we dreamed a dream in one night, I and he; we dreamed each man according to the interpretation of his dream.* **12** *And there was there with us a young man, an Hebrew, servant to the captain of the guard; and we told him, and he interpreted to us our dreams; to* *each man according to his dream he did interpret.* **13** *And it came to pass, as he interpreted to us, so it was; me he restored unto mine office, and him he hanged.* **14** *Then Pharaoh sent and called Joseph, and they brought him hastily out of the dungeon: and he shaved himself, and changed his raiment, and came in unto Pharaoh.* **15** *And Pharaoh said unto Joseph, I have dreamed a dream, and there is none that can interpret it: and I have heard say of thee, that thou canst understand a dream to interpret it.* **16** *And Joseph answered Pharaoh, saying, It is not in me: God shall give Pharaoh an answer of peace.*

There is a figure of speech that we often use to describe things finally changing from bad to good. We say, "It looks like the tide is turning." That is a very good way to describe it. Just think about it: when that tide is going out, when the water is rushing away, there is nothing in this world that can stop it. Man thinks he is so powerful, but if he is, let's see him stop the tide from going out! No one can stop it, not with bombs, sandbags, laws – it's impossible. But at just the right moment, just the way that God designed it, the tide turns, and starts coming back in, and once again, there is no way to stop it, you may as well just ride the wave.

Life had been pretty miserable for Joseph thus far. His brothers hated him, stole his colored coat, cast him into a pit and ate lunch while he begged for mercy, then sold him into slavery. Potiphar's wife lied about him, and he went to prison as an attempted rapist. Then while in prison, he really helped a man out and asked the man to return the favor when he got back to being Pharaoh's butler, and the guy chose to forget all about him. So Joseph spent two more long, lonely years in prison, while the tide of his life headed out.

But thank God, that tide got just so low but no lower. At just the right time God had that tide turn and from Genesis 41 on everything was very different for Joseph.

A Good Delay

Genesis 41:1a *And it came to pass at the end of two full years...*

This could not have seemed like a good delay to Joseph. If you are in prison for something you did not do how many days of that time are good? But God had a great plan for

Joseph, this two year delay was part of it, and that makes it a good delay.

It was two years for Pharaoh to start dreaming. This king's name was Apophis. Apophis had many very good nights of sleep. But God waited till he started dreaming to tell him of Joseph.

It was two more years for Joseph's brothers to get comfortable in the illusion that they had gotten by with their sin.

Above all, it was two more years for Joseph to be alone with God, learning all of the things he would need as second in command of Egypt: patience, administration, wisdom.

If God's timing is perfect, then any "delay" is a good delay!

A Grievous Dream
Genesis 41:1 *And it came to pass at the end of two full years, that Pharaoh dreamed: and, behold, he stood by the river. 2 And, behold, there came up out of the river seven well favoured kine and fatfleshed; and they fed in a meadow. 3 And, behold, seven other kine came up after them out of the river, ill favoured and leanfleshed; and stood by the other kine upon the brink of the river. 4 And the ill favoured and leanfleshed kine did eat up the seven well favoured and fat kine. So Pharaoh awoke.*

The river spoken of here was the Nile, the life-blood of Egypt. Without the Nile overflowing her banks each year, Egypt would not exist; it would be just a sandbox in the sun. So any dream that had anything to do with the Nile was sure to get the Pharaoh's attention!

In this dream, Pharaoh saw seven cows come up out of the river. They were good, very good. Large, fat, healthy, well-fed, perfect for grilling, with a basting of butter, salt, and pepper. Then seven "lean" ones came out and they devoured the good ones! Amazingly though, the bad cows did not improve after their consumption of the good ones. That dream was so troubling, Pharaoh woke up, but then he fell asleep once more.

Genesis 41:5 *And he slept and dreamed the second time: and, behold, seven ears of corn came up upon one stalk, rank and good. 6 And, behold, seven thin ears and blasted with* *the east wind sprung up after them. 7 And the seven thin ears devoured the seven rank and full ears. And Pharaoh awoke, and, behold, it was a dream.*

Pharaoh could not have missed the similarities between these dreams, nor could he escape the fact that no matter how you looked at it, the meaning could not possibly be good.

Genesis 41:8 *And it came to pass in the morning that his spirit was troubled; and he sent and called for all the magicians of Egypt, and all the wise men thereof: and Pharaoh told them his dream; but there was none that could interpret them unto Pharaoh.*

These men were supposed to be able to handle things just like this, but they couldn't. They were trained, they were educated, they had their "honorary doctorates," but they were helpless. It would take a slave from the prison house to provide the answer.

A Great Delivery

When I call this a great delivery, I mean it was a GREAT delivery, and in just a few minutes, you will see the amazing reason why.

Genesis 41:9 *Then spake the chief butler unto Pharaoh, saying, I do remember my faults this day:*

One cannot help but notice that he did not remember it until there was some possible benefit to him. As long as he had nothing to gain, he did not remember. It wasn't until he could be a hero by remembering that he did. A principle to remember and live by is this: Do right even when there is no "profit" in it! Joseph surely must have wished that the chief butler adhered to that principle.

And now, are you ready for something jaw-dropping? Let me ask you this: who was Potiphar? The Captain of the Guard. Do you know where Joseph went to prison when Mrs. Potiphar lied about him? Look at verse ten:

Genesis 41:10 *Pharaoh was wroth with his servants, and put me in ward in the captain of the guard's house, both me and the chief baker:*

That is where Joseph was! Twice in these chapters it is described as a dungeon, and now we find out it was a dungeon in that very place. Joseph was underneath Mr. and Mrs.

Potiphar's house. You would have had to literally go right through their house to get to that prison. Oh reader, just hold that thought for a moment. The Butler continued:

Genesis 41:11 *And we dreamed a dream in one night, I and he; we dreamed each man according to the interpretation of his dream.* **12** *And there was there with us a young man, an Hebrew, servant to the captain of the guard; and we told him, and he interpreted to us our dreams; to each man according to his dream he did interpret.* **13** *And it came to pass, as he interpreted to us, so it was; me he restored unto mine office, and him he hanged.*

This deed that Joseph did, the Butler forgot to reward him for it. In our flesh, so void of real understanding, it is tempting to ask why God would let that happen. But ask this instead: who would you rather have reward you, the butler, or the Pharaoh?

Genesis 41:14 *Then Pharaoh sent and called Joseph, and they brought him hastily out of the dungeon: and he shaved himself, and changed his raiment, and came in unto Pharaoh.*

Imagine this, let it sink in! They came and knocked on Potiphar's door to get Joseph. Imagine that scene. Mr. and Mrs. Potiphar are just getting out of bed, milling about the house, preparing for the day. Mr. Potiphar is at the table, eating a piece of buttered bread and reading his copy of the *Alexandria Times*. The home team took a drubbing the night before, losing to the Goshen Gophers 7 to 3. Mrs. Potiphar is still in curlers, she has not put on the day's makeup, and Mr. Potiphar cannot help but notice that she really, really needs to. Suddenly, a loud, insistent knocking is heard on the front door, followed by a gruff voice demanding, "Open up in the name of Apophis, Pharaoh of Egypt!"

Mr. Potiphar spits his orange juice halfway across the room in shock, and Mrs. Potiphar stands there dumbfounded, not daring to move or breathe. Potiphar gets up, opens the door, and three royal guards march in. One of them looks at Mrs. Potiphar, standing there in curlers and a robe, with her splotchy morning face and a serious bed-head. It is clear that he is unimpressed, to say the least. Then the leader announces his purpose. Potiphar is to go at once to the dungeon and bring forth a prisoner, who is to be immediately cleaned up, arrayed in royal robes, and brought before Pharaoh. Potiphar gulps, and asks which prisoner could possibly be so important. And then Mrs. Potiphar gulps, gulps, and gulps again when the name "Joseph, the Hebrew" falls off of the head guard's lips.

Within minutes, Joseph is brought right back up into the house, right in front of the woman who lied about him and got him thrown into prison, cleaned up, arrayed in royal robes, and brought to Pharaoh. Oh yes, you know that woman was sweating bullets.

The chickens, they do come home to roost!

Genesis 41:15 *And Pharaoh said unto Joseph, I have dreamed a dream, and there is none that can interpret it: and I have heard say of thee, that thou canst understand a dream to interpret it.* **16** *And Joseph answered Pharaoh, saying, It is not in me: God shall give Pharaoh an answer of peace.*

This was the boldest of gambles. Joseph stood before a pagan king, the man who held his life in his hands, a believer in many gods, none of them real, and spoke of the one true God. It is that kind of character that made the real God of Heaven to cause the tide to turn.

Chapter 9
Improbable, Impossible, Par for God's Course

Genesis 41:17 *And Pharaoh said unto Joseph, In my dream, behold, I stood upon the bank of the river:* **18** *And, behold, there came up out of the river seven kine, fatfleshed and well favoured; and they fed in a meadow:* **19** *And, behold, seven other kine came up after them, poor and very ill favoured and leanfleshed, such as I never saw in all the land of Egypt for badness:* **20** *And the lean and the ill favoured kine did eat up the first seven fat kine:* **21** *And when they had eaten them up, it could not be known that they had eaten them; but they were still ill favoured, as at the beginning. So I awoke.* **22** *And I saw in my dream, and, behold, seven ears came up in one stalk, full and good:* **23** *And, behold, seven ears, withered, thin, and blasted with the east wind, sprung up after them:* **24** *And the thin ears devoured the seven good ears: and I told this unto the magicians; but there was none that could declare it to me.* **25** *And Joseph said unto Pharaoh, The dream of Pharaoh is one: God hath shewed Pharaoh what he is about to do.* **26** *The seven good kine are seven years; and the seven good ears are seven years: the dream is one.* **27** *And the seven thin and ill favoured kine that came up after them are seven years; and the seven empty ears blasted with the east wind shall be seven years of famine.* **28** *This is the thing which I have spoken unto Pharaoh: What God is about to do he sheweth unto Pharaoh.* **29** *Behold,* *there come seven years of great plenty throughout all the land of Egypt:* **30** *And there shall arise after them seven years of famine; and all the plenty shall be forgotten in the land of Egypt; and the famine shall consume the land;* **31** *And the plenty shall not be known in the land by reason of that famine following; for it shall be very grievous.* **32** *And for that the dream was doubled unto Pharaoh twice; it is because the thing is established by God, and God will shortly bring it to pass.* **33** *Now therefore let Pharaoh look out a man discreet and wise, and set him over the land of Egypt.* **34** *Let Pharaoh do this, and let him appoint officers over the land, and take up the fifth part of the land of Egypt in the seven plenteous years.* **35** *And let them gather all the food of those good years that come, and lay up corn under the hand of Pharaoh, and let them keep food in the cities.* **36** *And that food shall be for store to the land against the seven years of famine, which shall be in the land of Egypt; that the land perish not through the famine.* **37** *And the thing was good in the eyes of Pharaoh, and in the eyes of all his servants.* **38** *And Pharaoh said unto his servants, Can we find such a one as this is, a man in whom the Spirit of God is?* **39** *And Pharaoh said unto Joseph, Forasmuch as God hath shewed thee all this, there is none so discreet and wise as thou art:* **40** *Thou shalt be over my house, and according unto thy word shall all my people be ruled: only in the throne will I be greater than thou.* **41** *And Pharaoh said unto Joseph, See, I have set thee over all the land of Egypt.* **42** *And Pharaoh took off his ring from his hand, and put it upon Joseph's hand, and arrayed him in vestures of fine linen, and put a gold chain about his neck;* **43** *And he made him to ride in the second chariot which he had; and they cried before him, Bow the knee: and he made him ruler over all the land of Egypt.* **44** *And Pharaoh said unto Joseph, I am Pharaoh, and without thee shall no man lift up his hand or foot in all the land of Egypt.* **45** *And Pharaoh called Joseph's name Zaphnathpaaneah; and he gave him to wife Asenath the daughter of Potipherah priest of On. And Joseph went out over all the land of Egypt.* **46** *And Joseph was thirty years old when he stood before Pharaoh king of Egypt. And Joseph went out from the presence of Pharaoh, and went throughout all the land of Egypt.*

With men, many things are impossible. With God, the impossible becomes commonplace! That will be demonstrated again and again in this episode from the life of Joseph.

The Warning of Pharaoh

Genesis 41:17 *And Pharaoh said unto Joseph, In my dream, behold, I stood upon the bank of the river:* **18** *And, behold, there came up out of the river seven kine, fatfleshed and well favoured; and they fed in a meadow:* **19** *And, behold, seven other kine came up after them, poor and very ill favoured and leanfleshed, such as I never saw in all the land of Egypt for badness:* **20** *And the lean and the ill favoured kine did eat up the first seven fat kine:* **21** *And when they had eaten them up, it could not be known that they had eaten them; but they were still ill favoured, as at the beginning. So I awoke.*

There are quite a few things of which to take note in these verses.

Notice, to begin with, that these cows came up out of the river. It may seem unusual, for cows to be coming up out of the river, but the message fit perfectly. Life itself in Egypt came up out of the Nile. No Nile -- no water, no water -- no food, no food -- no life.

Secondly, see that the bad cows weren't just bad; they were the worst he had ever seen. They were designed to be harbingers of a famine so bad, the world itself would be affected.

Thirdly, bad cows ate up good cows, left no trace of them, and yet were in no way improved or fattened by their voluminous consumption. Again, that cannot have any kind of a positive meaning.

Genesis 41:22 *And I saw in my dream, and, behold, seven ears came up in one stalk, full and good:* **23** *And, behold, seven ears, withered, thin, and blasted with the east wind, sprung up after them:* **24** *And the thin ears devoured the seven good ears: and I told this unto the magicians; but there was none that could declare it to me.*

This is the same dream, only with different details. One detail, though, is not simply a re-statement, but an additional piece of information. We are told of the east wind, which sweeps over the deserts of Arabia, picking up a head of steam and intense heat and wipes out everything in its path. This was a great warning of how things were going to be like for Egyptian farmers. The warning was made more ominous by the fact that the men who were trained to interpret such dreams could not!

Genesis 41:25 *And Joseph said unto Pharaoh, The dream of Pharaoh is one: God hath shewed Pharaoh what he is about to do.* **26** *The seven good kine are seven years; and the seven good ears are seven years: the dream is one.* **27** *And the seven thin and ill favoured kine that came up after them are seven years; and the seven empty ears blasted with the east wind shall be seven years of famine.*

Famine was the most feared of all words, there must have been a collective gasp in the court when that word was uttered by Joseph.

Genesis 41:28 *This is the thing which I have spoken unto Pharaoh: What God is about to do he sheweth unto Pharaoh.* **29** *Behold, there come seven years of great plenty throughout all the land of Egypt:* **30** *And there shall arise after them seven years of famine; and all the plenty shall be forgotten in the land of Egypt; and the famine shall consume the land;* **31** *And the plenty shall not be known in the land by reason of that famine following; for it shall be very grievous.* **32** *And for that the dream was doubled unto Pharaoh twice; it is because the thing is established by God, and God will shortly bring it to pass.*

The specter of the famine was made more ominous by the warning from Joseph that there would be no chance to avoid it and not much time to get ready for it either. This warning was ominous, awful, devastating.

Joseph had given Pharaoh all he asked for. But now, he had enough sense to do more. The wise men and magicians had not had the sense to interpret the dream, so why should they be the ones to come up with the solution? This was perhaps the wisest and riskiest thing that Joseph ever did, the Hebrew slave boldly giving counsel to the Egyptian Pharaoh.

The Wisdom of Joseph

Genesis 41:33 *Now therefore let Pharaoh look out a man discreet and wise, and set him over the land of Egypt.*

The words of Joseph were wise and true. Seek not a committee; seek a man. Seek not one who is popular; seek one who is discreet and wise.

Genesis 41:34 *Let Pharaoh do this, and let him* **(the man Pharaoh appoints)** *appoint officers over the land, and take up the fifth part of the land of Egypt in the seven plenteous years.* **35** *And let them gather all the food of those good years that come, and lay up corn under the hand of Pharaoh, and let them keep food in the cities.* **36** *And that food shall be for store to the land against the seven years of famine, which shall be in the land of Egypt; that the land perish not through the famine.* **37** *And the thing was good in the eyes of Pharaoh, and in the eyes of all his servants.*

This was ingenious and also historically groundbreaking. It changed the structure of a nation, which we will cover in greater detail later. It also established a principle that our own government would be wise to follow -- have a flat rate, twenty percent tax, and let the rich, middle class, and poor, all pay that same rate. And then from those tax proceeds, let government save volumes during the good times in anticipation of the bad times.

This plan established the power of Pharaoh. Up to this point, provincial nobles had held most of the power and had not done very well with it. Unfortunately, years later this change would haunt the Israelites.

The Working of God

Genesis 41:38 *And Pharaoh said unto his servants, Can we find such a one as this is, a man in whom the Spirit of God is?*

When Pharaoh spoke of the Spirit of God, the words are *Ruach Elohim*, the exact same words used in Genesis 1:2. They may not have accepted Him, but they knew Him!

Genesis 41:39 *And Pharaoh said unto Joseph, Forasmuch as God hath shewed thee all this, there is none so discreet and wise as thou art:*

These are the exact same words Joseph used, discreet and wise. It is instructive to note that Joseph simply stated the proper qualifications, without ever saying or inferring that he himself possessed them. Let another's lips praise thee, and not thine own!

Genesis 41:40 *Thou shalt be over my house, and according unto thy word shall all my people be ruled: only in the throne will I be greater than thou.* **41** *And Pharaoh said unto Joseph, See, I have set thee over all the land of Egypt.* **42** *And Pharaoh took off his ring from his hand, and put it upon Joseph's hand, and arrayed him in vestures of fine linen, and put a gold chain about his neck;* **43** *And he made him to ride in the second chariot which he had; and they cried before him, Bow the knee: and he made him ruler over all the land of Egypt.* **44** *And Pharaoh said unto Joseph, I am Pharaoh, and without thee shall no man lift up his hand or foot in all the land of Egypt.* **45** *And Pharaoh called Joseph's name Zaphnathpaaneah* **(revealer of secrets)***; and he gave him to wife Asenath the daughter of Potipherah priest of On. And Joseph went out over all the land of Egypt.* **46** *And Joseph was thirty years old when he stood before Pharaoh king of Egypt. And Joseph went out from the presence of Pharaoh, and went throughout all the land of Egypt.*

In an instant, Joseph had a new name, a wife, freedom, control, and power. Bow the knee! Do you think Joseph ever thought he would hear these words, spoken in this way? Even his teenage dream could not have fully prepared him for the impact of this moment.

Chapter 10
The Day the Stars Bowed Down

Genesis 41:47 *And in the seven plenteous years the earth brought forth by handfuls.* **48** *And he gathered up all the food of the seven years, which were in the land of Egypt, and laid up the food in the cities: the food of the field, which was round about every city, laid he up in the same.* **49** *And Joseph gathered corn as the sand of the sea, very much, until he left numbering; for it was without number.* **50** *And unto Joseph were born two sons before the years of famine came, which Asenath the daughter of Potipherah priest of On bare unto him.* **51** *And Joseph called the name of the firstborn Manasseh: For God, said he, hath made me forget all my toil, and all my father's house.* **52** *And the name of the second called he Ephraim: For God hath caused me to be fruitful in the land of my affliction.* **53** *And the seven years of plenteousness, that was in the land of Egypt, were ended.* **54** *And the seven years of dearth began to come, according as Joseph had said: and the dearth was in all lands; but in all the land of Egypt there was bread.* **55** *And when all the land of Egypt was famished, the people cried to Pharaoh for bread: and Pharaoh said unto all the Egyptians, Go unto Joseph; what he saith to you, do.* **56** *And the famine was over all the face of the earth: And Joseph opened all the storehouses, and sold unto the Egyptians; and the famine waxed sore in the land of Egypt.* **57** *And all countries came into Egypt to Joseph for to buy corn; because that the famine was so sore in all lands.*

Genesis 42:1 *Now when Jacob saw that there was corn in Egypt, Jacob said unto his sons, Why do ye look one upon another?* **2** *And he said, Behold, I have heard that there is corn in Egypt: get you down thither, and buy for us from thence; that we may live, and not die.* **3** *And Joseph's ten brethren went down to buy corn in Egypt.* **4** *But Benjamin, Joseph's brother, Jacob sent not with his brethren; for he said, Lest peradventure mischief befall him.* **5** *And the sons of Israel came to buy corn among those that came: for the famine was in the land of Canaan.* **6** *And Joseph was the governor over the land, and he it was that sold to all the people of the land: and Joseph's brethren came, and bowed down themselves before him with their faces to the earth.* **7** *And Joseph saw his brethren, and he knew them, but made himself strange unto them, and spake roughly unto them; and he said unto them, Whence come ye? And they said, From the land of Canaan to buy food.* **8** *And Joseph knew his brethren, but they knew not him.* **9** *And Joseph remembered the dreams which he dreamed of them...*

Way back in his teenage years Joseph dreamed a dream in which the sun, moon, and stars, representing his father, mother, and brothers, would bow down to him. His brothers scoffed, sneered, and swore that it would never happen.

The Preparation for the Future

Genesis 41:47 *And in the seven plenteous years the earth brought forth by handfuls.* **48** *And he gathered up all the food of the seven years, which were in the land of Egypt, and laid up the food in the cities: the food of the field, which was round about every city, laid he up in the same.* **49** *And Joseph gathered corn as the sand of the sea, very much, until he left numbering; for it was without number.*

Years of plenty do not last for ever. Years of plenty are the best time to lie up for the lean years. In this case, if you remember, the savings rate was twenty percent. Further wisdom was shown in that what was saved was also diversified. It was stored in cities, plural. So much was saved, in fact, that Joseph could not even number it.

This pattern would save a great many homes from divorce and our nation itself from financial ruin. The overwhelming majority of couples that I have counseled, who are near the brink of divorce, have a single thing in common -- stress brought on by their own financial mismanagement. Unfortunately, many of these couples were married by Bible-believing Baptist pastors, who never took the time to thoroughly counsel them on issues that could destroy them, such as how they handle (or mishandle) their money! Pastors, counsel those that you marry, especially on areas as vital as finances. Couples, before you marry, seek out that counseling. If your own pastor will not or cannot do it, seek that counsel from some godly person who can and will!

The Proper Choice of Attitude
    Genesis 41:50 *And unto Joseph were born two sons before the years of famine came, which Asenath the daughter of Potipherah priest of On bare unto him.* **51** *And Joseph called the name of the firstborn Manasseh: For God, said he, hath made me forget all my toil, and all my father's house.* **52** *And the name of the second called he Ephraim: For God hath caused me to be fruitful in the land of my affliction.* **53** *And the seven years of plenteousness, that was in the land of Egypt, were ended.*

    The World War II generation is commonly called "The Greatest Generation." I believe, if we were to be accurate, ours could be called "The Whiniest Generation." People who have reasons to pout and mope, do. People who do not have reasons to pout and mope, do as well! It is a rare thing indeed to find anymore a person who has reasons to whine and mope, yet does not. Joseph was such a man.

    In the midst of a tragic life, a life robbed of everything, Joseph chose the right attitude, and that attitude is reflected in the names of his sons. Mannaseh's name indicated that God had been so good to Joseph in the midst of all of his tragedies, that Joseph had forgotten all of the agony he had been through. Ephraim's name indicated that in the midst of affliction, God had still been good and had made Joseph fruitful and prosperous. In addition to being good reminders to Joseph, those names would also serve as good teaching tools for the children. What better attitude can a parent instill in his children than an attitude of gratefulness in every circumstance!

The Power of Hunger

Genesis 41:54 *And the seven years of dearth began to come, according as Joseph had said: and the dearth was in all lands; but in all the land of Egypt there was bread.* **55** *And when all the land of Egypt was famished, the people cried to Pharaoh for bread: and Pharaoh said unto all the Egyptians, Go unto Joseph; what he saith to you, do.* **56** *And the famine was over all the face of the earth: And Joseph opened all the storehouses, and sold unto the Egyptians; and the famine waxed sore in the land of Egypt.* **57** *And all countries came into Egypt to Joseph for to buy corn; because that the famine was so sore in all lands.*

The tool box of God is large and well-stocked with a diversity of effective instruments. In this instance, God used hunger to move the brothers of Joseph to go into Egypt. Hunger will get you where God wants you eventually!

The Promise Fulfilled

Genesis 42:1 *Now when Jacob saw that there was corn in Egypt, Jacob said unto his sons, Why do ye look one upon another?*

What a mental picture -- Reuben looking at Simeon because he was hungry, Levi looking at Naphtali. It reminds me of the old Tweety and Sylvester cartoons, where a starving Sylvester would be watching Tweety on his swing in the cage, and Tweety would suddenly be a big ham-hock swinging in front of him.

Genesis 42:2a *And he said, Behold, I have heard that there is corn in Egypt:*

The good news of life-giving food does travel!

Genesis 42:2b *...get you down thither, and buy for us from thence; that we may live, and not die.* **3** *And Joseph's ten brethren went down to buy corn in Egypt.* **4** *But Benjamin, Joseph's brother, Jacob sent not with his brethren; for he said, Lest peradventure mischief befall him.*

Something should leap out to the thoughtful reader of Scripture at this point. Why did Joseph's brothers hate him and sell him into slavery? They were jealous because the father loved him better than them. So they "fixed" their problem by sinning, selling their own brother into Egypt.

But lo and behold, what do we now find? Benjamin has taken Joseph's place as the favored child. They did not "fix" their problem by sinning! They still were in the exact same boat, only the brother changed. Sin will never fix your problem.

Genesis 42:5 *And the sons of Israel came to buy corn among those that came: for the famine was in the land of Canaan.* **6** *And Joseph was the governor over the land, and he it was that sold to all the people of the land: and Joseph's brethren came, and bowed down themselves before him with their faces to the earth.* **7** *And Joseph saw his brethren, and he knew them, but made himself strange unto them, and spake roughly unto them; and he said unto them, Whence come ye? And they said, From the land of Canaan to buy food.* **8** *And Joseph knew his brethren, but they knew not him.* **9** *And Joseph remembered the dreams which he dreamed of them...*

"Joseph, are you mad? You snotty little dreamer, we will never, NEVER come and bow down to you!"

"Look, here comes the Dreamer! Let's cast him into a pit and see what will become of his dreams..."

"What is that? A caravan! Ishmeelites and Midianites. We won't make a profit by killing Joseph; let's sell him into slavery. That way, we can put some change in our pockets, and ensure that we never have to bow down to Joseph. He'll spend the rest of his life bowing down to heathens!"

"We're so sorry to have to show you this, Father. It looks like Joseph's coat, and it is torn to shreds, covered in blood. Is this his coat? Do you think this means that he is dead?"

"We got by with it! It's been years now. No Joseph, no colored coat, and no chance of us ever having to bow down to him. He's probably dead by now, there's little chance he would have survived this many years as a slave in Egypt."

"We're hungry, Father! The famine has swept the land, all of the grass is dead, the crops are gone, we're all going to starve unless we go into Egypt to buy food!"

"There he is, the Egyptian in charge of selling food. Everyone hurry now, all of us need to bow down before him."

And that was the day that the stars bowed down...

Chapter 11
And One Is Not

Genesis 42:9 *And Joseph remembered the dreams which he dreamed of them, and said unto them, Ye are spies; to see the nakedness of the land ye are come.* **10** *And they said unto him, Nay, my lord, but to buy food are thy servants come.* **11** *We are all one man's sons; we are true men, thy servants are no spies.* **12** *And he said unto them, Nay, but to see the nakedness of the land ye are come.* **13** *And they said, Thy servants are twelve brethren, the sons of one man in the land of Canaan; and, behold, the youngest is this day with our father, and one is not.* **14** *And Joseph said unto them, That is it that I spake unto you, saying, Ye are spies:* **15** *Hereby ye shall be proved: By the life of Pharaoh ye shall not go forth hence, except your youngest brother come hither.* **16** *Send one of you, and let him fetch your brother, and ye shall be kept in prison, that your words may be proved, whether there be any truth in you: or else by the life of Pharaoh surely ye are spies.* **17** *And he put them all together into ward three days.* **18** *And Joseph said unto them the third day, This do, and live; for I fear God:* **19** *If ye be true men, let one of your brethren be bound in the house of your prison: go ye, carry corn for the famine of your houses:* **20** *But bring your youngest brother unto me; so shall your words be verified, and ye shall not die. And they did so.* **21** *And they said one to another, We are verily guilty concerning our brother, in that we saw the anguish of his soul, when he besought us, and we would not hear; therefore is this distress* *come upon us.* **22** *And Reuben answered them, saying, Spake I not unto you, saying, Do not sin against the child; and ye would not hear? therefore, behold, also his blood is required.* **23** *And they knew not that Joseph understood them; for he spake unto them by an interpreter.* **24** *And he turned himself about from them, and wept; and returned to them again, and communed with them, and took from them Simeon, and bound him before their eyes.*

Joseph has gone from a little boy who was daddy's favorite, to a teenager despised by his brothers and sold into slavery, to a household servant in Egypt who was falsely accused of attempted rape. He has been in prison, he has been forgotten by those he befriended and helped. He has been called out of that prison to stand before Pharaoh to interpret a dream, and has become the man in charge of all Egypt. He has become the human savior of the world, the one man who had enough wisdom to keep the world from starving to death during an awful famine of seven years time.

During all of that, Joseph never forgot that God had promised to make his brothers come and bow down before him. And as we saw in the last chapter, that is exactly what happened. Spurred on by their own growling stomachs, these men found themselves in Egypt to buy food. The man in charge of selling it knew them, but they didn't know him. These brothers bowed themselves to the ground before Joseph, the one thing they all swore they would never do.

That is where we left off last time. As we begin this new section, my mind is drawn to one thing these boys said. When Joseph accused them of being spies, look how they answered him in verse thirteen:

Genesis 42:13 *And they said, Thy servants are twelve brethren, the sons of one man in the land of Canaan; and, behold, the youngest is this day with our father, and one is not.*

Who was that one that they said "was not?" That would be Joseph.

Shaking the Stars

In the dream of Joseph many years before, these brothers had been stars. That was good with them, they loved the idea of being bright, shining, noticeable. They loved it right up to the point where Joseph said, in effect, "Stars or not, you are going to bow before me, God told me so." That part they didn't like even a little. Now here they are in Egypt, still proud, still haughty. After all these years, they still need to be "shaken" really well and Joseph is now in a position to do it.

Genesis 42:9 *And Joseph remembered the dreams which he dreamed of them, and said unto them, Ye are spies; to see the nakedness of the land ye are come.*

That was the most fearsome of accusations. These men knew that they could be executed on the spot. They could be imprisoned and cast into some desolate pit. Does that sound familiar? It did to them! Years before, Joseph had been sent to "spy" on them, and they cast him into a pit, and then sold him into slavery. Now they are on the verge of having the exact same thing happen to them.

Genesis 42:10 *And they said unto him, Nay, my lord, but to buy food are thy servants come.*

It is amazing how quickly people can learn humility. They had NEVER been so humble and polite in their entire lives!

Genesis 42:11 *We are all one man's sons; we are true men, thy servants are no spies.*

When Joseph accused them of being spies, they had an obvious answer for him. "No sir, we aren't a bunch of guys from different families and places, coming to check you out and then bring in troops against you. In fact, we're all from the same family, we're all brothers. Just look at us, can't you see the resemblance?"

This is exactly what Joseph needed for them to answer; I'll show you why in just a moment. For now, he needed to push them a little farther.

Genesis 42:12 *And he said unto them, Nay, but to see the nakedness of the land ye are come.*

Nakedness is used here as a synonym for "defenseless." Joseph was saying, "You think we're weak because of this famine. You're spies, seeing how best to overthrow us." He has really sold them on the idea that they are going to be quickly imprisoned or killed. So, desperate, they try one more time to convince him, and this time they go a little farther than before:

Genesis 42:13 *And they said, Thy servants are twelve brethren, the sons of one man in the land of Canaan; and, behold, the youngest is this day with our father, and one is not.*

Joseph's precious mother, Rachel, had died many years before. She died while giving birth to Joseph's baby brother, Benjamin. The brothers had hated Joseph, mostly because Daddy loved him so much. Daddy loved him so much because he loved Rachel so much. So if these boys had been so cruel to Joseph, what was the way that they would likely have treated Benjamin? Much of Joseph's approach was designed to find out about Benjamin, without giving away who he was. That worked. He now knows that Benjamin is alive and safe with Daddy.

But what he probably did not expect was for them to reference Joseph himself. They said, "We are all brothers, there are twelve of us, ten of us here, the youngest back home with daddy, and oh, I guess we should have said that we are eleven brothers, because one is not." They really believed that they had gotten rid of Joseph forever! What must their conversations have been like, years after they sold him, as they sat around their campfires? "Yep, Joseph's gone for good. I guarantee you, he's dead by now. Some slave master has killed him for us."

They told Joseph, "One is not," when the one they were talking to was the one that they said "isn't" any more!

What did God say in **Numbers 32:23**? *Be sure your sins will find you out...*

Genesis 42:14 *And Joseph said unto them, That is it that I spake unto you, saying, Ye are spies:* **15** *Hereby ye shall be proved: By the life of Pharaoh ye shall not go forth hence, except your youngest brother come hither.* **16** *Send one of you, and let him fetch your brother, and ye shall be kept in prison, that your words may be proved, whether there be any truth in you: or else by the life of Pharaoh surely ye are spies.* **17** *And he put them all together into ward three days.*

This is just a fitting and beautiful thing. Joseph is doing an excellent job putting the squeeze on these men. After they are done telling about the family, thinking that will convince this awesome ruler before them, he says, "I was right when I said you were spies. But if you're not, I'll give you a way to prove it. I'll throw all of you but one into prison. You decide who gets to go home. Whoever goes gets to bring back this 'brother' you claim to have. You have three days to figure out who goes."

And then he threw them into prison, walked away, and left them to sweat. If I know Joseph, I bet he put them into the same prison where he himself had been held!

Seeking a Brother
Genesis 42:18 *And Joseph said unto them the third day, This do, and live; for I fear God:* **19** *If ye be true men, let one of your brethren be bound in the house of your prison: go ye, carry corn for the famine of your houses:* **20** *But bring your youngest brother unto me; so shall your words be verified, and ye shall not die. And they did so.*

I mentioned in the very first chapter that Joseph is a beautiful picture of Christ Himself in so many ways. Here is another example of that. Joseph had originally planned to keep all but one of them, so that the one could go get Benjamin. But during their three days of confinement, he changed his plan, choosing to keep just one and let the others go. Why? In Joseph's words, so that the ones going home could "carry corn for the famine of your houses." It dawned on Joseph that the family back home was starving and needed food, much more food than one person could carry. So he chose to send all but one of them back, and make them all come back, bringing Benjamin, which is exactly what they later did.

Stirring the Memory
Genesis 42:21 *And they said one to another, We are verily guilty concerning our brother, in that we saw the anguish of his soul, when he besought us, and we would not hear; therefore is this distress come upon us.*

While speaking to the brothers, Joseph had been speaking through an interpreter. He had been speaking Egyptian, rather than Hebrew, to avoid giving away who he was. They thought that he couldn't understand them. So as they are muttering among themselves in Hebrew, they start talking about why all of this is happening, and Joseph, unknown to them, understands what they are saying. What he heard let him know something very clearly: for twenty years, their consciences had been eating away at them night and day. The very first thing they thought of when trouble hit was "God is judging us for what we did to Joseph!"

I guarantee you they never expected this. People who do wrong always seem to think that once they're done, it's over. But God has placed a cruel task master into the human mind, a thing called conscience. When you do wrong, not only will God judge you if you are lost or chasten you if you are saved, but you will have a voice in your heart and head screaming at you night and day. Your conscience can drive you insane. In fact, a great many people are on heavy medication, anti-depressants, and mood altering drugs just trying to find some relief from the nagging voice of conscience. If you have done wrong, you don't need drugs, you need to make things right!

Genesis 42:22 *And Reuben answered them, saying, Spake I not unto you, saying, Do not sin against the child; and ye would not hear? therefore, behold, also his blood is required.*

This had to be a cross between a hug and a kick in the gut to Joseph. He never knew about this part. He did not know that Reuben had tried to find a way to deliver him. That happened in Genesis 37:21-22, and it happened while Joseph was still a great way off, and they were making plans what to do to him. Reuben tried to find a way to save Joseph. He managed to save his life, but he was away from the pit when the others sold him into slavery. Joseph was already gone by the time Reuben got back to the pit. Reuben rent his clothes and wept that Joseph was gone. All those years, twenty solid years, Joseph thought that all of his older brothers were in on this, that all were glad to have him gone. Joseph never knew until this point that his oldest brother had actually tried to save him. That explains what happened next:

Genesis 42:23 *And they knew not that Joseph understood them; for he spake unto them by an interpreter.* **24a** *And he turned himself about from them, and wept...*

Can you imagine the emotional roller coaster that Joseph was on? After all these years, he found out that he did have at least one brother who cared enough to try and help him. That just broke Joseph; he had to excuse himself and find a private place to cry. He had stirred their memories, but he had his own stirred up as well.

Securing Collateral

Genesis 42:24b *...and returned to them again, and communed with them, and took from them Simeon, and bound him before their eyes.*

Do you wonder why Joseph chose Simeon? I submit to you that five minutes earlier, he would have chosen Reuben. Here's why I say that: Reuben was the firstborn, and as such, in charge of all the rest. He had to act the part of the mean brother at that pit, to satisfy the rest of them while he looked for a way to free Joseph. But before he could do that, Joseph was sold by the rest. He spent the next twenty years believing that Reuben was in charge of all that happened. But now he knows better. So who was in charge, then? That would be the next oldest boy. That would be Simeon.

So Joseph, knowing what he now knows, reaches out and grabs Simeon. Twenty years earlier, the roles had been reversed. Twenty years earlier, Simeon had reached out and grabbed and bound him. Now, all these years later, Joseph grabs Simeon, and the rest have to watch helplessly as he slaps him in shackles and hauls him away. Twenty years earlier, Joseph had been separated from his brothers by Simeon. Now Simeon is separated from his brothers by Joseph.

But that isn't all. Sin always takes more than you may think it deserves. According to Genesis 46:10, Simeon by this time had six children of his own. He has had time to grow up, have kids, and fall in love with them. He has bounced them on his knee and hugged them tight. And as far as he knows, as he is being dragged into this Egyptian prison, he is never going to see them again.

I don't know what sin you, Dear Reader, are involved in, but whatever it is, I do know this -- it will cost you far, far more than you ever thought it would.

Chapter 12
Is There Any "Fun" in "Dysfunctional?"

Genesis 42:25 *Then Joseph commanded to fill their sacks with corn, and to restore every man's money into his sack, and to give them provision for the way: and thus did he unto them.* **26** *And they laded their asses with the corn, and departed thence.* **27** *And as one of them opened his sack to give his ass provender in the inn, he espied his money; for, behold, it was in his sack's mouth.* **28** *And he said unto his brethren, My money is restored; and, lo, it is even in my sack: and their heart failed them, and they were afraid, saying one to another, What is this that God hath done unto us?* **29** *And they came unto Jacob their father unto the land of Canaan, and told him all that befell unto them; saying,* **30** *The man, who is the lord of the land, spake roughly to us, and took us for spies of the country.* **31** *And we said unto him, We are true men; we are no spies:* **32** *We be twelve brethren, sons of our father; one is not, and the youngest is this day with our father in the land of Canaan.* **33** *And the man, the lord of the country, said unto us, Hereby shall I know that ye are true men; leave one of your brethren here with me, and take food for the famine of your households, and be gone:* **34** *And bring your youngest brother unto me: then shall I know that ye are no spies, but that ye are true men: so will I deliver you your brother, and ye shall traffick in the land.* **35** *And it came to pass as they emptied their sacks, that, behold, every man's bundle of money was in his sack: and when both they and their father saw the bundles of money, they were afraid.* **36** *And*

Jacob their father said unto them, Me have ye bereaved of my children: Joseph is not, and Simeon is not, and ye will take Benjamin away: all these things are against me. **37** *And Reuben spake unto his father, saying, Slay my two sons, if I bring him not to thee: deliver him into my hand, and I will bring him to thee again.* **38** *And he said, My son shall not go down with you; for his brother is dead, and he is left alone: if mischief befall him by the way in the which ye go, then shall ye bring down my gray hairs with sorrow to the grave.*

Genesis 43:1 *And the famine was sore in the land.* **2** *And it came to pass, when they had eaten up the corn which they had brought out of Egypt, their father said unto them, Go again, buy us a little food.* **3** *And Judah spake unto him, saying, The man did solemnly protest unto us, saying, Ye shall not see my face, except your brother be with you.* **4** *If thou wilt send our brother with us, we will go down and buy thee food:* **5** *But if thou wilt not send him, we will not go down: for the man said unto us, Ye shall not see my face, except your brother be with you.* **6** *And Israel said, Wherefore dealt ye so ill with me, as to tell the man whether ye had yet a brother?* **7** *And they said, The man asked us straitly of our state, and of our kindred, saying, Is your father yet alive? have ye another brother? and we told him according to the tenor of these words: could we certainly know that he would say, Bring your brother down?* **8** *And Judah said unto Israel his father, Send the lad with me, and we will arise and go; that we may live, and not die, both we, and thou, and also our little ones.* **9** *I will be surety for him; of my hand shalt thou require him: if I bring him not unto thee, and set him before thee, then let me bear the blame for ever:* **10** *For except we had lingered, surely now we had returned this second time.* **11** *And their father Israel said unto them, If it must be so now, do this; take of the best fruits in the land in your vessels, and carry down the man a present, a little balm, and a little honey, spices, and myrrh, nuts, and almonds:* **12** *And take double money in your hand; and the money that was brought again in the mouth of your sacks, carry it again in your hand; peradventure it was an oversight:* **13** *Take also your brother, and arise, go again unto the man:* **14** *And God Almighty give you mercy before the man, that he may send away your other* *brother, and Benjamin. If I be bereaved of my children, I am bereaved.*

In the last chapter, Joseph had bound Simeon and imprisoned him before the eyes of his brothers. He had told them that in order to have Simeon freed, and in order to be able to buy any more food, they had to bring Benjamin back with them.

There is a fairly modern word that we now use to describe families that we once would have just called "weird." That word is "dysfunctional." Why have we adopted such a nice sounding word for weird? I'll tell you why: we all looked around at our own families and realized that most of them fit into the "weird" category in some way! So, since we were all afflicted, we had no trouble agreeing to "nicen things up a bit."

Are you a member of a family that is dysfunctional in some way? Joseph certainly was. And in this text, that dysfunction, that weirdness, is on full display. This family demonstrated dysfunction is several ways.

Blaming God for Their Troubles

Genesis 42:25 *Then Joseph commanded to fill their sacks with corn, and to restore every man's money into his sack, and to give them provision for the way: and thus did he unto them.*

Joseph had grown into a man with a flair for the dramatic. His brothers had bowed down to him. He, as the second in command of Egypt, could have brought the full weight of his authority down upon them that very moment. But instead he chose another approach. The brothers had come with money to buy food. That money had been given to the proper people under Joseph. But when Joseph had their sacks filled with corn, he also instructed his servants to put all of their money back into their sacks without their knowledge.

Genesis 42:27 *And as one of them opened his sack to give his ass provender in the inn, he espied his money; for, behold, it was in his sack's mouth.* **28a** *And he said unto his brethren, My money is restored; and, lo, it is even in my sack: and their heart failed them...*

Had Joseph simply desired to do these men a kindness, he would have given the money back to them personally, so that they would be aware of it. It was not his intention to do them a kindness. His purpose was to make them nervous every single moment till they got back and faced him again, his purpose was to make sure that every waking moment was spent thinking of the fearsome man in charge of Egypt.

His plan worked beautifully! The text says that "their heart failed them." It means that their hearts skipped beats, had spasms, and went completely irregular! These men truly, literally, almost had heart attacks when they saw the money in their sacks.

And what was their response to this latest trial?

Genesis 42:28b *...and they were afraid, saying one to another, What is this that God hath done unto us?*

It is doubtless the height of dysfunction to sin, experience the consequences of that sin, and then blame God for one's troubles! But their dysfunction was only beginning. They also showed it:

Building Trust in "Odd" Ways

Genesis 42:29 *And they came unto Jacob their father unto the land of Canaan, and told him all that befell unto them; saying,* **30** *The man, who is the lord of the land, spake roughly to us, and took us for spies of the country.* **31** *And we said unto him, We are true men; we are no spies:* **32** *We be twelve brethren, sons of our father; one is not, and the youngest is this day with our father in the land of Canaan.* **33** *And the man, the lord of the country, said unto us, Hereby shall I know that ye are true men; leave one of your brethren here with me, and take food for the famine of your households, and be gone:* **34** *And bring your youngest brother unto me: then shall I know that ye are no spies, but that ye are true men: so will I deliver you your brother, and ye shall traffick in the land.* **35** *And it came to pass as they emptied their sacks, that, behold, every man's bundle of money was in his sack: and when both they and their father saw the bundles of money, they were afraid.*

The brothers had seen the money already, now they are seeing it again, and yet their fear has not diminished! Father Jacob has his own fear added to the mix and then adds his voice as well:

Genesis 42:36 *And Jacob their father said unto them, Me have ye bereaved of my children: Joseph is not, and Simeon is not, and ye will take Benjamin away: all these things are against me.*

It is in verse 36 that we gain some insight into the mind and thoughts of Jacob. Jacob said, "Me have ye bereaved of my **children**," and then he names Simeon and Joseph. Benjamin is still there and is not included in the list of those of whom he is bereaved. Benjamin is mentioned as the one whom he fears will be taken from him. This lets us know that Jacob, though he had no proof of their involvement, held them responsible for the "death" of Joseph. He suspected that they were involved! He did not blame an accident; he blamed them.

Genesis 42:37 *And Reuben spake unto his father, saying, Slay my two sons, if I bring him not to thee: deliver him into my hand, and I will bring him to thee again.*

Please follow the reasoning and argumentation of Reuben. "Dad, I know you are worried that if you send Benjamin with us, you may never see him again. Let me give you a good reason to trust us with your youngest son. If we don't bring him back, you can kill my two sons, your two grandsons!" With such assurance, who would not have full confidence and trust in a man like Reuben?

The dysfunction continued. Now we see them:

Burying Their Heads in the Sand

Genesis 42:38 *And he said, My son shall not go down with you; for his brother is dead, and he is left alone: if mischief befall him by the way in the which ye go, then shall ye bring down my gray hairs with sorrow to the grave.*

Allow me to present a paraphrase of what Jacob just said: "You are not taking my son Benjamin down into Egypt! If you do, he *might* just die somehow along the way. I am keeping that boy right here so that we can all definitely die of starvation!"

Perhaps the reader is not convinced as yet that Jacob is indeed putting his head in the sand, and becoming willfully oblivious to the situation. The next two verses will drive home the point more forcefully:

Genesis 43:1 *And the famine was sore in the land.* **2** *And it came to pass, when they had eaten up the corn which they had brought out of Egypt, their father said unto them, Go again, buy us a little food.*

Not, "We have no choice, take Benjamin with you and go buy food," but simply, "Go again and buy us a little food." No mention of Simeon, no mention of Benjamin, no mention of the money in the sacks, and no mention of the fierce ruler who is expecting them to return with their youngest brother.

Genesis 43:3 *And Judah spake unto him, saying, The man did solemnly protest unto us, saying, Ye shall not see my face, except your brother be with you.* **4** *If thou wilt send our brother with us, we will go down and buy thee food:* **5** *But if thou wilt not send him, we will not go down: for the man said unto us, Ye shall not see my face, except your brother be with you.*

Judah, the fourth born, the man who in chapter 38 of Genesis demonstrated decidedly poor character, now begins to assert himself in an impressive manner. He, it seems, alone among the brothers, has the insight and ability to realize the gravity of the situation and to convince his father of it as well. When difficult situations arise, either of our own making or not, a good rule of thumb is "head up, eyes open."

We further see the family demonstrating their dysfunction by:

Behaving in the Same Way that Caused the Trouble to Start With

Genesis 43:11 *And their father Israel said unto them, If it must be so now, do this; take of the best fruits in the land in your vessels, and carry down the man a present, a little balm, and a little honey, spices, and myrrh, nuts, and almonds:* **12** *And take double money in your hand; and the money that was brought again in the mouth of your sacks, carry it again in your hand; peradventure it was an oversight:* **13** *Take also your brother, and arise, go again unto the man:* **14** *And God Almighty give you mercy before the man, that he may send away your other brother, and Benjamin. If I be bereaved of my children, I am bereaved.*

In most of what Jacob said there is great and practical wisdom. He first of all instructed his children to prepare a gift to take to Egypt with them to give to the fierce young ruler. Many years later, Solomon would give inspired testimony to the wisdom of this action:

Proverbs 21:14 *A gift in secret pacifieth anger: and a reward in the bosom strong wrath.*

Jacob, though he did not have the ability to look into the future and read this wisdom of Solomon, did have the ability to look into the past, his past, and know that the approach was effective. Many years before, he had come before his angry brother Esau after a twenty year absence, and sent a great gift before him to pacify his brother. The fact that he was still alive reminded him that it had worked, and may well work again for his sons.

But it is after his wise instruction to bring the gifts that we see his foolish dysfunction in behaving in the same way that caused the trouble to start with. Notice verse 14 once again.

Genesis 43:14 *And God Almighty give you mercy before the man, that he may send away your other brother, and Benjamin. If I be bereaved of my children, I am bereaved.*

Your other brother... and Benjamin. The "other brother" had a name! Father Jacob does not think enough of Simeon to even speak his name, but when it comes to Joseph's younger brother, Rachel's only remaining son, he calls him Benjamin. The favoritism that so infuriated the brothers years earlier has not disappeared, it has strengthened and transferred to Benjamin.

Chapter 13
Don't You Know?

Genesis 43:15 *And the men took that present, and they took double money in their hand, and Benjamin; and rose up, and went down to Egypt, and stood before Joseph.* **16** *And when Joseph saw Benjamin with them, he said to the ruler of his house, Bring these men home, and slay, and make ready; for these men shall dine with me at noon.* **17** *And the man did as Joseph bade; and the man brought the men into Joseph's house.* **18** *And the men were afraid, because they were brought into Joseph's house; and they said, Because of the money that was returned in our sacks at the first time are we brought in; that he may seek occasion against us, and fall upon us, and take us for bondmen, and our asses.* **19** *And they came near to the steward of Joseph's house, and they communed with him at the door of the house,* **20** *And said, O sir, we came indeed down at the first time to buy food:* **21** *And it came to pass, when we came to the inn, that we opened our sacks, and, behold, every man's money was in the mouth of his sack, our money in full weight: and we have brought it again in our hand.* **22** *And other money have we brought down in our hands to buy food: we cannot tell who put our money in our sacks.* **23** *And he said, Peace be to you, fear not: your God, and the God of your father, hath given you treasure in your sacks: I had your money. And he brought Simeon out unto them.* **24** *And the man brought the men into Joseph's house, and gave them water, and they washed their feet; and he gave their asses provender.* **25** *And they made* *ready the present against Joseph came at noon: for they heard that they should eat bread there.* **26** *And when Joseph came home, they brought him the present which was in their hand into the house, and bowed themselves to him to the earth.* **27** *And he asked them of their welfare, and said, Is your father well, the old man of whom ye spake? Is he yet alive?* **28** *And they answered, Thy servant our father is in good health, he is yet alive. And they bowed down their heads, and made obeisance.* **29** *And he lifted up his eyes, and saw his brother Benjamin, his mother's son, and said, Is this your younger brother, of whom ye spake unto me? And he said, God be gracious unto thee, my son.* **30** *And Joseph made haste; for his bowels did yearn upon his brother: and he sought where to weep; and he entered into his chamber, and wept there.* **31** *And he washed his face, and went out, and refrained himself, and said, Set on bread.* **32** *And they set on for him by himself, and for them by themselves, and for the Egyptians, which did eat with him, by themselves: because the Egyptians might not eat bread with the Hebrews; for that is an abomination unto the Egyptians.* **33** *And they sat before him, the firstborn according to his birthright, and the youngest according to his youth: and the men marvelled one at another.* **34** *And he took and sent messes unto them from before him: but Benjamin's mess was five times so much as any of theirs. And they drank, and were merry with him.*

In the last chapter, Jacob and his sons argued over whether they would return to Egypt for more food. Their argument centered around the fact that Joseph had demanded that they bring Benjamin back with them. Simeon had been languishing in an Egyptian prison for months, while Jacob refused to send Benjamin. It was Judah who finally persuaded his father, Jacob. He basically said, "Father, that man told us that we couldn't buy so much as one more grain of corn unless Benjamin came back with us. You're worried about losing him if we take him into Egypt, but if we don't take him into Egypt with us, you're going to lose him anyway, because he's going to starve to death, and so are all the rest of us."

Hearing that reasoning, Jacob finally had to agree. So he told the boys to take double money back with them, since they had found their money still in their sacks when they got back last time, and they were also to take some little gifts for that fierce ruler that they didn't yet recognize as Joseph. That is where we will pick things back up.

The Trip Back into Egypt
Genesis 43:15 *And the men took that present, and they took double money in their hand, and Benjamin; and rose up, and went down to Egypt, and stood before Joseph.*

As these men returned down to Egypt, they carried three things with them: a present (the spices), a payment (the money), and a promise (their brother). All of these things were good. It is good to bring a present to people, it is a sign of thoughtfulness. It is definitely good to pay your bills.

But truthfully, Joseph couldn't have cared less about the spices or the money. All he cared about was seeing his little brother.

The Terror at Mealtime
Genesis 43:16 *And when Joseph saw Benjamin with them, he said to the ruler of his house, Bring these men home, and slay, and make ready; for these men shall dine with me at noon.* **17** *And the man did as Joseph bade; and the man brought the men into Joseph's house.*

It is amazing to me to consider the steely nerves of Joseph. Up until this point, whenever his brothers had been in front of him, he had very carefully spoken Egyptian, speaking to them through an interpreter. But you would think that now, finally seeing Benjamin, he would slip up.

Not Joseph. Joseph calmly turned to his servant, and in flawless Egyptian, told him to bring these men to his house for lunch. Then, it seems from the context, he walked away to tend to other business.

The servant turned to the men, and did not ask them, but told them that they were going to eat at Joseph's house at noon.

Can you imagine how terrifying this would be? Every experience they have had with him has been harsh and costly. All they want is to get into Egypt, get Simeon, get food, and get gone. But they now know that isn't going to happen. The next verse shows just how scared they were:

Genesis 43:18 *And the men were afraid, because they were brought into Joseph's house; and they said, Because of the money that was returned in our sacks at the first time are we brought in; that he may seek occasion against us, and fall upon us, and take us for bondmen, and our asses.*

Adam Clark made this great statement: "A guilty conscience needs no accuser, for everything alarms them."[1]

Look at the assumptions these men automatically made. First we are being brought to his house because of the money that was still in our sacks. He thinks we're thieves!

Second, he is bringing us to lunch to get us to slip up somehow.

Third, he wants to take us for slaves.

Fourth, he even wants to take all of our pack animals.

Now here is the thing, none of these assumptions made any sense. If Joseph thought they were thieves, he would never have allowed them into his home; he would have arrested them on the spot. He wasn't trying to get them to slip up; he was in charge of all Egypt, he didn't have to wait for them to slip up. He didn't want to take them as slaves, otherwise he would never have let them go the first time. And what need did he have of pack animals? He wasn't going anywhere, and he was already insanely wealthy.

So why did they automatically jump to these scary conclusions? Because again, a guilty conscience needs no accuser, for everything alarms them. If you have any sense, you will not do anything to give yourself a guilty conscience. A guilty conscience makes for sleepless nights and days filled with worry.

Genesis 43:19 *And they came near to the steward of Joseph's house, and they communed with him at the door of the house,* **20** *And said, O sir, we came indeed down at the first time to buy food:* **21** *And it came to pass, when we came to the inn, that we opened our sacks, and, behold, every man's money was in the mouth of his sack, our money in full weight: and we have brought it again in our hand.* **22** *And other money have we brought down in our hands to buy food: we cannot tell who put our money in our sacks.*

It is interesting to observe that for once, these men were completely, totally honest. Why is it that they had to be scared to death in order to tell the truth?

But another thing I notice here is that they were too frightened to approach Joseph himself with this, so they went to his servant instead. Joseph had done a very good job making himself terribly intimidating to them.

Genesis 43:23 *And he said, Peace be to you, fear not: your God, and the God of your father, hath given you treasure in your sacks: I had your money. And he brought Simeon out unto them.*

This is the first moment in Egypt that these men saw any glimmer of a ray of hope. The steward says, "Don't worry about it. I am the one who put that money in your sacks. And by the way, this gift is really from your God, the God of your fathers. He hasn't forgotten about you for even a moment." And then he brought Simeon out to them. They thought that they were going to end up in prison with him, and instead, they find him set at liberty.

The Thin Disguise

This is the part of this passage that I have been wanting to get to. It is these eleven verses that make me title it "Don't You Know?" As we go through this, I want you to pay attention to something. Up till now, Joseph has done everything possible to not drop any clue about his identity and not leave a single hint.

But not at this meal. Watch with me as to how many clues he drops and all that he does to get them to figure out who he is.

Genesis 43:24 *And the man brought the men into Joseph's house, and gave them water, and they washed their feet; and he gave their asses provender.* **25** *And they made ready the present against Joseph came at noon: for they heard that they should eat bread there.*

Joseph's brothers are now cleaned up, their animals are taken care of, and they have carefully prepared the presents to give to him when he gets there, still not even knowing that it is their little brother they are going to be giving them to.

Genesis 43:26 *And when Joseph came home, they brought him the present which was in their hand into the house, and bowed themselves to him to the earth.*

Do you remember all of the gifts that they brought him? For Joseph, this was like a trip down memory lane. It was a bunch of the herbs and spices and honey that he had grown up eating in the land of Canaan. How many years had it been since he had enjoyed any of that? And I wonder how Joseph managed to keep from laughing as they presented each one and told him what it was and how good it was?

And then you see these brothers once again doing what they swore they would never do -- bowing down their faces to the earth before Joseph.

Genesis 43:27 *And he asked them of their welfare, and said, Is your father well, the old man of whom ye spake? Is he yet alive?* **28** *And they answered, Thy servant our father is in good health, he is yet alive. And they bowed down their heads, and made obeisance.*

This is the first thing that should have given the identity of Joseph away. There was no reason at all that a mighty foreign leader should be concerned about their old father. Who would logically be the only person on earth other than them who would really be concerned about Jacob? That would be Jacob's missing son, Joseph. If he really wanted to keep his identity hidden, he would not have asked about Jacob.

Genesis 43:29 *And he lifted up his eyes, and saw his brother Benjamin, his mother's son, and said, Is this your younger brother, of whom ye spake unto me? And he said, God be gracious unto thee, my son.*

Once again, Joseph dropped some significant clues as to his identity in this verse. He showed particular affection for Benjamin. Why? You say, "Because Benjamin was a precious little kid." Wrong answer. Benjamin was a fully grown adult, and according to Genesis 46:21, he already had ten children of his own by this time!

So the affection that Joseph showed for him really should have been a dead giveaway.

But notice as well that Joseph said to Benjamin, "God be gracious to you, My Son." The word he used for God was the Hebrew word Elohim. This was no Egyptian god he was referring to, it was not Ra, or Osiris, or Sutekh, it was the God of the Hebrews, that Joseph, if he really were an Egyptian, should not have known or regarded.

Genesis 43:30 *And Joseph made haste; for his bowels did yearn upon his brother: and he sought where to weep; and he entered into his chamber, and wept there.* **31** *And he washed his face, and went out, and refrained himself, and said, Set on bread.*

Joseph wanted to hug his little brother so badly he couldn't stand it. He wanted to cry like a baby on his shoulder. But he didn't want to do that till his brothers figured it out. So instead, he went into a room and cried for a while, then composed himself and came back out. Then he commanded for the meal to begin, and when it did the clues just kept on coming.

Genesis 43:32 *And they set on for him by himself, and for them by themselves, and for the Egyptians, which did eat with him, by themselves: because the Egyptians might not eat bread with the Hebrews; for that is an abomination unto the Egyptians.*

This seating arrangement was another dead giveaway. If Joseph wanted to hide his identity, he would never have let them eat with him, because of what they would see. When the meal was set on, there was not one big group sitting all together. There was all of the Egyptians sitting by themselves, all of the brothers sitting by themselves, and then Joseph sitting by himself. Everyone knew that the Egyptians would not sit at the same table as a Hebrew. If Joseph was really an Egyptian, why would the others not sit with him, or he with them?

But the next clue really should have gotten them. Please remember that we are talking about eleven full grown adults, with kids of their own. If you look at a family of eleven grown up children, how successful do you think you would be at guessing their birth order, oldest to youngest? But look at the next verse.

Genesis 43:33 *And they sat before him, the firstborn according to his birthright, and the youngest according to his youth: and the men marvelled one at another.*

Joseph arranged all of this. He had them seated in the proper order of their birth, oldest to youngest. Who was the only person on earth, other than their family back home, that could possibly have done this? Joseph!

Now look at one last clue.

Genesis 43:34 *And he took and sent messes unto them from before him: but Benjamin's mess was five times so much as any of theirs. And they drank, and were merry with him.*

Joseph directed his servants to give plates of food to all of the brothers. But after the first ten were served, when it came time for Benjamin, the last, he sent five times as much as he did to any of the others.

Who on earth would do that? Who would be the only person with any motivation to show favoritism to Benjamin? The only person on earth would be his long lost brother Joseph.

As the passage closes, they are all having a wonderful good time, but they still haven't figured it out yet. It still just hasn't clicked. You can almost see Joseph dying inside, thinking, "My brothers, don't you know? Can't you figure it out? How many more clues do I need to drop?"

This is another example of the fact that Joseph is a beautiful type of Christ. If He desired to do so, the Lord Jesus Christ could miraculously appear in our midst, walk up to any of us, slap us on the forehead, and say, "It's me! I'm the Lord God that you are supposed to be worshiping."

But if God did that, He would be establishing a one-way relationship, where He does all of the work, all of the seeking, and puts in all of the effort. That has never been the desire of God. It has always been His desire not only to seek us, but to get us to seek Him as well:

Jeremiah 29:13 *And ye shall seek me, and find me, when ye shall search for me with all your heart.*

Isaiah 55:6 *Seek ye the LORD while he may be found, call ye upon him while he is near:*

You say, "But what clues has He left me? What has He done to let me know who He is?" Have you ever heard of Bethlehem? The wilderness temptation? Gethsemene? Pilate's judgement hall? Calvary? The empty tomb?

Don't you know?

Chapter 14
The Rise of Judah

Genesis 44:1 *And he commanded the steward of his house, saying, Fill the men's sacks with food, as much as they can carry, and put every man's money in his sack's mouth.* **2** *And put my cup, the silver cup, in the sack's mouth of the youngest, and his corn money. And he did according to the word that Joseph had spoken.* **3** *As soon as the morning was light, the men were sent away, they and their asses.* **4** *And when they were gone out of the city, and not yet far off, Joseph said unto his steward, Up, follow after the men; and when thou dost overtake them, say unto them, Wherefore have ye rewarded evil for good?* **5** *Is not this it in which my lord drinketh, and whereby indeed he divineth? ye have done evil in so doing.* **6** *And he overtook them, and he spake unto them these same words.* **7** *And they said unto him, Wherefore saith my lord these words? God forbid that thy servants should do according to this thing:* **8** *Behold, the money, which we found in our sacks' mouths, we brought again unto thee out of the land of Canaan: how then should we steal out of thy lord's house silver or gold?* **9** *With whomsoever of thy servants it be found, both let him die, and we also will be my lord's bondmen.* **10** *And he said, Now also let it be according unto your words: he with whom it is found shall be my servant; and ye shall be blameless.* **11** *Then they speedily took down every man his sack to the ground, and opened every man his sack.* **12** *And he searched, and began at the eldest, and left at the youngest: and the cup was found in*

Benjamin's sack. **13** *Then they rent their clothes, and laded every man his ass, and returned to the city.* **14** *And Judah and his brethren came to Joseph's house; for he was yet there: and they fell before him on the ground.* **15** *And Joseph said unto them, What deed is this that ye have done? wot ye not that such a man as I can certainly divine?* **16** *And Judah said, What shall we say unto my lord? what shall we speak? or how shall we clear ourselves? God hath found out the iniquity of thy servants: behold, we are my lord's servants, both we, and he also with whom the cup is found.* **17** *And he said, God forbid that I should do so: but the man in whose hand the cup is found, he shall be my servant; and as for you, get you up in peace unto your father.* **18** *Then Judah came near unto him, and said, Oh my lord, let thy servant, I pray thee, speak a word in my lord's ears, and let not thine anger burn against thy servant: for thou art even as Pharaoh.* **19** *My lord asked his servants, saying, Have ye a father, or a brother?* **20** *And we said unto my lord, We have a father, an old man, and a child of his old age, a little one; and his brother is dead, and he alone is left of his mother, and his father loveth him.* **21** *And thou saidst unto thy servants, Bring him down unto me, that I may set mine eyes upon him.* **22** *And we said unto my lord, The lad cannot leave his father: for if he should leave his father, his father would die.* **23** *And thou saidst unto thy servants, Except your youngest brother come down with you, ye shall see my face no more.* **24** *And it came to pass when we came up unto thy servant my father, we told him the words of my lord.* **25** *And our father said, Go again, and buy us a little food.* **26** *And we said, We cannot go down: if our youngest brother be with us, then will we go down: for we may not see the man's face, except our youngest brother be with us.* **27** *And thy servant my father said unto us, Ye know that my wife bare me two sons:* **28** *And the one went out from me, and I said, Surely he is torn in pieces; and I saw him not since:* **29** *And if ye take this also from me, and mischief befall him, ye shall bring down my gray hairs with sorrow to the grave.* **30** *Now therefore when I come to thy servant my father, and the lad be not with us; seeing that his life is bound up in the lad's life;* **31** *It shall come to pass, when he seeth that the lad is not with us, that he will die: and thy servants shall bring down the gray hairs of thy servant our father with sorrow to the grave.* **32** *For* *thy servant became surety for the lad unto my father, saying, If I bring him not unto thee, then I shall bear the blame to my father for ever.* **33** *Now therefore, I pray thee, let thy servant abide instead of the lad a bondman to my lord; and let the lad go up with his brethren.* **34** *For how shall I go up to my father, and the lad be not with me? lest peradventure I see the evil that shall come on my father.*

Have you ever stopped to think of how significant Judah is in Scripture? Just consider the numbers related to these twelve brothers. Joseph is mentioned 228 times. Reuben 74 times. Levi 72. Simeon 50. Asher 43. Gad 72. Dan 72. Naphthali 50. Zebulun 45. Issachar 44. Benjamin 162. Altogether the eleven brothers of Judah are mentioned 912 times in Scripture. Judah is mentioned 813 times all by himself!

Jesus came through Judah. Revelation 5:5 calls Jesus the Lion of the tribe of Judah. Judah rose far above his brethren and this passage is where he began to do so.

Verses 1 through 15 present Joseph laying one final trial at his brothers' feet. Let's walk through these verses one by one. At the end, in verse 14 these men will be called "Judah and his brethren." At the end, Judah rises...

He Rose When He Acknowledged Their Guilt
Genesis 44:16a *And Judah said, What shall we say unto my lord? what shall we speak? or how shall we clear ourselves? God hath found out the iniquity of thy servants...*

Judah was saying, "Sir, there is nothing we can say..."

But isn't that interesting? Couldn't he have said, "We didn't steal it! I don't know who put it there, but it wasn't us!" For Judah, the answer was no, and here is why. He finally figured out that what was happening to them had nothing to do with the present and everything to do with the past. This wasn't about the money in their sack; it was about the money they got for selling Joseph. It wasn't about some silver cup that a human could "see things" with; it was about the God of Heaven who saw what they did to their brother. Judah knew and acknowledged that God was fighting against them because they were guilty.

Sinner Friend, you may have some good deeds here and there, but that won't stop God from fighting against you, because you are guilty!

Back-slidden Christian, doing a few good deeds won't get God off your back. You better make things right, quickly! Attempting to cover or deny one's sin is a sure recipe for disaster:

Proverbs 28:13 *He that covereth his sins shall not prosper: but whoso confesseth and forsaketh them shall have mercy.*

Judah chose to acknowledge the sin that had for so long been carefully concealed.

He Rose When He Stopped Taking the Escape Route

Genesis 44:10 *And he said, Now also let it be according unto your words: he with whom it is found shall be my servant; and ye shall be blameless.*

Compare this verse with verse 16.

Genesis 44:16 *And Judah said, What shall we say unto my lord? what shall we speak? or how shall we clear ourselves? God hath found out the iniquity of thy servants: behold, we are my lord's servants, both we, and he also with whom the cup is found.*

The steward of Joseph gave them a green light to run. They never had to see that fierce ruler again! They were cleared to leave on the spot; they didn't have to go back to Joseph's house. But with Judah now running the show, every one of them went back. When they got there, Joseph gave them another chance to run:

Genesis 44:17 *And he said, God forbid that I should do so: but the man in whose hand the cup is found, he shall be my servant; and as for you, get you up in peace unto your father.*

And how did Judah respond to this second temptation?

Genesis 44:18a *Then Judah came near unto him...*

Judah is in the midst of the greatest danger, and he will not take the escape route, because his brother and father are depending on him. Judah ran towards trouble, rather than away from it, just like One from his line would do so many years later, running towards a cross rather than away from it.

He Rose When He Was Willing to Risk Everything to Save Another

Genesis 44:18 *Then Judah came near unto him, and said, Oh my lord, let thy servant, I pray thee, speak a word in my lord's ears, and let not thine anger burn against thy servant: for thou art even as Pharaoh.*

What was he saying? "I know you could kill me for even approaching you, but I'm going to take the chance, because the life of another depends on it." This was the first time in the record of these men that any of them took thought for one of the others. Their lives up till this point had shown a consistent pattern of self-centeredness, caring not a whit for others. Judah rose *above* his brothers because he became willing to lay down his life *for* his brothers.

He Rose When He Was Willing to Take All the Responsibility for Future Results upon Himself

In verses 19 through 23, Judah recounted for Joseph, word for word, what their last conversation was like:

Genesis 44:19 *My lord asked his servants, saying, Have ye a father, or a brother?* **20** *And we said unto my lord, We have a father, an old man, and a child of his old age, a little one; and his brother is dead, and he alone is left of his mother, and his father loveth him.* **21** *And thou saidst unto thy servants, Bring him down unto me, that I may set mine eyes upon him.* **22** *And we said unto my lord, The lad cannot leave his father: for if he should leave his father, his father would die.* **23** *And thou saidst unto thy servants, Except your youngest brother come down with you, ye shall see my face no more.*

And then in verses 24 through 29, he told Joseph what he did not know: he told him how things went when they got back home the last time after their meeting with him.

Genesis 44:24 *And it came to pass when we came up unto thy servant my father, we told him the words of my lord.* **25** *And our father said, Go again, and buy us a little food.* **26** *And we said, We cannot go down: if our youngest brother be with us, then will we go down: for we may not see the man's face, except our youngest brother be with us.* **27** *And thy servant my father said unto us, Ye know that my wife bare me two sons:* **28** *And the one went out from me, and I said, Surely he is torn in* *pieces; and I saw him not since:* **29** *And if ye take this also from me, and mischief befall him, ye shall bring down my gray hairs with sorrow to the grave.*

And then we come to verses 30 through 31, where Judah takes responsibility for future results upon himself.

Genesis 44:30 *Now therefore when I come to thy servant my father, and the lad be not with us; seeing that his life is bound up in the lad's life;* **31** *It shall come to pass, when he seeth that the lad is not with us, that he will die: and thy servants shall bring down the gray hairs of thy servant our father with sorrow to the grave.*

He could have said, "Sir, if you keep Benjamin, you are going to kill my father." But he didn't. He said, "If daddy dies, Sir, it will be our fault, my fault." That is taking responsibility in its fullest sense, and it is something that his wicked brothers never did.

He Rose When He Remembered and Kept a Commitment

Genesis 44:32 *For thy servant became surety for the lad unto my father, saying, If I bring him not unto thee, then I shall bear the blame to my father for ever.*

This is something that Joseph did not know. Can you imagine what it was like for him to hear this? This man thought enough of my baby brother that he became the personal surety for his safe return! This man, who participated in selling me into Egypt, has changed to such a degree that he has made a personal commitment to bring my brother Benjamin back home. Joseph could see that the years had wrought a remarkable change in Judah! Many people make commitments. Far fewer actually remember and keep them.

He Rose When He Stepped Out and Requested to Be Enslaved Instead of Benjamin

Genesis 44:33 *Now therefore, I pray thee, let thy servant abide instead of the lad a bondman to my lord; and let the lad go up with his brethren.*

Any of the brothers could have offered this. There was nothing at all to prevent Reuben from doing it, or Simeon or Levi or any of them. But only Judah did. In fact, Reuben and Simeon and Levi, by dint of being elder than Judah, should have stepped up before him and made this offer. But it was Judah who cared enough for his brother and his father to offer himself in exchange for Benjamin. Years later, his father Jacob would say this of him:

Genesis 49:8 *Judah, thou art he whom thy brethren shall praise: thy hand shall be in the neck of thine enemies; thy father's children shall bow down before thee.*

His brethren did indeed praise him, and we, his spiritual brothers, continue to do so to this day.

He Rose When He Stopped Trying to Make the Father Happy Without the Son

Genesis 44:34 *For how shall I go up to my father, and the lad be not with me? lest peradventure I see the evil that shall come on my father.*

Years earlier the brothers established a pattern of attempting to please the father without the son.

Genesis 37:35 *And all his sons and all his daughters rose up to comfort him; but he refused to be comforted; and he said, For I will go down into the grave unto my son mourning. Thus his father wept for him.*

They did their best, their very best, to comfort their old father in Joseph's absence. They knew where Joseph was, they knew how to get him back, but they intentionally tried to satisfy the father without him.

This is yet another example of Joseph being an excellent picture of Christ! It is Christ, and Christ alone, that is able to satisfy the Father:

Isaiah 53:11 *He shall see of the travail of his soul, and shall be satisfied: by his knowledge shall my righteous servant justify many; for he shall bear their iniquities.*

1 John 2:2 *And he is the propitiation* **(the satisfaction)** *for our sins: and not for ours only, but also for the sins of the whole world.*

Judah learned something that made him rise far above all of his brothers. You will never, ever make the Father happy without the Son.

Chapter 15
I Am Joseph

Genesis 45:1 *Then Joseph could not refrain himself before all them that stood by him; and he cried, Cause every man to go out from me. And there stood no man with him, while Joseph made himself known unto his brethren.* **2** *And he wept aloud: and the Egyptians and the house of Pharaoh heard.* **3** *And Joseph said unto his brethren, I am Joseph; doth my father yet live? And his brethren could not answer him; for they were troubled at his presence.*

He started out as the son that his father never thought he would have, a boy from the womb of his dear wife Rachel. He was so loved by his father, and as a result, so hated by his other ten brothers. He was the possessor of the precious many-colored coat and the recipient of prophetic dreams from God himself.

He was also a victim. His own flesh and blood, his brothers, determined to kill him. In the end, they settled for stripping him of his coat of many colors, casting him into a pit, selling him into slavery in a foreign land, and letting his father think he was dead.

But Joseph was also a blessed individual. He kept his character, and God continued to honor him, even as a slave in Egypt. Potiphar's wife tried to get him to sleep with her, and, knowing it was wrong, he refused. So she accused him of attempted rape and had him thrown into prison. He was only there for a few years before he found himself standing before the Pharaoh himself, interpreting a dream for him. Everything after that was an absolute whirlwind. In the blink of an eye, Joseph went from a prisoner to the second most powerful man on earth. He was the man with the plan for saving Egypt and the rest of the world from an incredible famine. It was that famine that brought ten very familiar faces before Joseph. They were older, more wrinkled and care-worn, but unmistakable nonetheless. They didn't recognize him, but he recognized them, and he used that to a great, great advantage. He imprisoned Simeon, and demanded that if they ever wanted to see him again, and if they wanted so much as another mouthful of food, they would bring their youngest brother Benjamin, whom they did not know was also his baby brother, back to Egypt with them. It took them a while to convince daddy Jacob, but when hunger finally got the best of them, they did just that.

When they got back, they didn't just get food, they got their money back, they got Simeon, and they got a wonderful meal and good fellowship in the house of Joseph. They left there feeling like the weight of the world was off of their shoulders. How re-assuring must it have been to think that if they ever needed anything, the second in command of all Egypt was now a friendly acquaintance.

That feeling of bliss was short lived. Not long after they left for home, the steward of Joseph caught up with them, and accused them of stealing Joseph's "magic silver cup." He then searched their bags, and found the cup (which he himself had planted) in Benjamin's bag. At that moment, their whole world fell apart. Joseph let them know that he would be keeping Benjamin as a slave, and the rest of them were free to go.

It was at that moment that one of the brothers finally showed some character. Judah stepped to the forefront, and offered to stay as a slave instead of Benjamin. It was that great act of selflessness that finally broke Joseph out of his disguise, and caused one of the greatest reunions in all of history.

Many times in this book we have observed what a wonderful type of Christ Joseph is. This text will be another incredible example of that.

The Desire of Joseph

Genesis 45:1a *Then Joseph could not refrain himself before all them that stood by him; and he cried, Cause every man to go out from me...*

Through most of their time together during their two meetings in Egypt, it was Joseph's desire to veil himself. This was so that the prophecy of Joseph's dreams could be fulfilled. His focus had been on portraying himself as a hard, strict ruler; but now, the son part of Joseph, and the brother part of Joseph, came gushing to the top. In fact, he could not help but to explode in a torrent of emotion. Because of this, he sent all the Egyptians out, crying, "Cause every man to go out from me!" What must that have been like for the Egyptians?

After all these years, Joseph now wants nothing more than to let his family know who he is. Can you see the picture of our soon reunion with Christ? He has been veiled to our eyes; we see Him through His Word, and through His dealings in our lives. We walk by faith, not by sight. But there is a soon-coming day, when we will walk by sight and not by faith. We will see Him! He will reveal Himself to us, we will be caught up together to meet Him in the air, and so shall we ever be with the Lord. This is our desire, but it is much more so His desire!

The Discomfort of a Solitary Meeting

Genesis 45:1 *Then Joseph could not refrain himself before all them that stood by him; and he cried, Cause every man to go out from me. And there stood no man with him, while Joseph made himself known unto his brethren.*

It is truly amazing how similar and yet completely different situations can be at the exact same time. This is not the first time that Joseph has been alone with his brothers. The last time he was alone with them, it was a very uncomfortable time... for him. The brothers held all of the power, he was helpless before them, his life and fate was in their hands. Now, all of these years later, he is once again alone with them, and the table is completely turned! He holds all the power, they are helpless before him, their lives and fates are in his hands. They have already trembled before him when he was but a fierce, unknown foreign ruler in their minds. But now he is a scorned, stripped, and sold brother with a legitimate grudge that has had years to fester. They dare not touch him, for all of the might and power of Egypt are his. A word from his mouth will result in their torture and death, and also for their entire family back home if he so desires. Never has any group of siblings felt so uncomfortable in the presence of one of their other siblings!

The Drama that Could Not Be Hidden

Genesis 45:2 *And he wept aloud: and the Egyptians and the house of Pharaoh heard.*

There is no indication in Scripture that, through the long years of his stay in Egypt, Joseph had told anyone the story of his family. But when he began to weep and wail, sobbing at the top of his lungs, it did not take long for the house of Pharaoh to hear. When the vice president cries aloud, the president, congress, and shortly thereafter, the population at large will hear of it.

That truth could not be comforting to the brothers. Pharaoh would hear, and matters would go from terrible to even more terrible! Why could this entire messy affair not simply be hidden away forever?

Their own experiences, and those of their father Jacob, should have taught them that sins do not remain hidden. Judah's fornication with Tamar became known when she became pregnant, Jacob's deception before his father Isaac became known when Esau arrived moments behind him, and Simeon and Levi's sin in slaughtering Shechem and the men of his city became so well known that their father feared that they would be made to stink before the inhabitants of the land.

The Delight of Reunion

Genesis 45:3a *And Joseph said unto his brethren, I am Joseph; doth my father yet live?*

Two things are striking to me here. First of all, his brothers had already told him, more than once, that the father was alive and well:

Genesis 43:26 *And when Joseph came home, they brought him the present which was in their hand into the house, and bowed themselves to him to the earth.* **27** *And he asked them of their welfare, and said, Is your father well, the old man* *of whom ye spake? Is he yet alive?* **28** *And they answered, Thy servant our father is in good health, he is yet alive...*

Genesis 44:18 *Then Judah came near unto him, and said, Oh my lord, let thy servant, I pray thee, speak a word in my lord's ears, and let not thine anger burn against thy servant: for thou art even as Pharaoh.* **19** *My lord asked his servants, saying, Have ye a father, or a brother?* **20** *And we said unto my lord, We have a father, an old man, and a child of his old age, a little one; and his brother is dead, and he alone is left of his mother, and his father loveth him.*

Genesis 44:34 *For how shall I go up to my father, and the lad be not with me? lest peradventure I see the evil that shall come on my father.*

Yet in spite of these repeated assurances that their father is alive and well, he is now asking again. He is fully aware of their dishonest character! He does not put it beyond them at all to have lied, repeatedly, about their own father's supposed well being. People of dishonest character should never be offended when their veracity is oft doubted!

The second thing that is striking is that Joseph had it all... but all he cared about was a reunion with the father. His power, wealth, prestige, position, wife, and sons could not quench his desire to be reunited with his father.

On Earth for thirty-three plus years, Jesus was God walking among men. He could have had anything at all He desired. His power was such that nothing was beyond His reach; no power, no pleasure, no profit, nothing. In addition, the devil himself at one point literally offered Him everything:

Matthew 4:8 *Again, the devil taketh him up into an exceeding high mountain, and sheweth him all the kingdoms of the world, and the glory of them;* **9** *And saith unto him, All these things will I give thee, if thou wilt fall down and worship me.*

Yet Jesus, who could have had it all, refused it all:

Matthew 4:10 *Then saith Jesus unto him, Get thee hence, Satan: for it is written, Thou shalt worship the Lord thy God, and him only shalt thou serve.*

What the Son desired was to complete the task that the Father had sent Him to do and then have a reunion with the Father. What must it have been like when He showed back up in Heaven!

The Distress of the Guilty

Genesis 45:3 *And Joseph said unto his brethren, I am Joseph; doth my father yet live? And his brethren could not answer him; for they were troubled at his presence.*

If it were possible for anything in the Bible to be labeled as an understatement, this would be it. They were "troubled" at his presence. This Hebrew word *bahal* means to be terrified, affrighted, alarmed, disturbed, anxious, nervous, dismayed. All that is wrapped up in that word "troubled."

Is it any wonder why? This isn't Joseph their helpless little brother anymore. This is their worst nightmare; this is Joseph, so all-powerful that he literally holds their very lives in his hands. Talk about the tables being turned! This is a long way from that pit where he was crying and begging for mercy.

But that scene is more than just a literal, historical event. It is also a foreshadowing of the day when we, the brothers of Christ, will face the Lord Jesus Christ. In II Corinthians 5:11 Paul called that meeting, which we know as the Judgment Seat of Christ, "The terror of the Lord…"

2 Corinthians 5:10 *For we must all appear before the judgment seat of Christ; that every one may receive the things done in his body, according to that he hath done, whether it be good or bad.*

As far as salvation is concerned, that debt was paid on Calvary and our sins are forever forgiven the moment we place our faith in Jesus Christ. But as far as reward and loss is concerned, we will one and all answer for the deeds done in our body, and those brethren who have done despite to Christ will be universally *bahal* -- terrified, affrighted, alarmed, disturbed, anxious, nervous, dismayed... troubled!

The Details of Their Surprise

These things now taking place as the brothers cowered before Joseph, God told them they would happen. He gave it to them by direct revelation that they would one day bow before Joseph whether they liked it or not. So why were they so surprised? For the exact same set of reasons that many other people will be surprised when they come face to face with the Jesus that they rejected while they had a chance to accept Him.

They thought he "was not."

Genesis 42:13 *And they said, Thy servants are twelve brethren, the sons of one man in the land of Canaan; and, behold, the youngest is this day with our father, and one is not.*

All of the paper and ink of Earth seemingly would not suffice to tell of the multitudes of people that now believe that Jesus "is not." The brothers behaved as they behaved and then were surprised at Joseph's presence, because they believed that they would never see him again. People behave as they behave -- drinking, fornicating, engaging in homosexuality and lesbianism, using drugs, cursing, committing adultery, lying, stealing, killing – because they believe that they will never have to face God; they think that He "is not."

He had been gone for a very long time.

Somewhere in the neighborhood of twenty years has elapsed! Or around two thousand years, depending on Who you're talking about:

2 Peter 3:3 *Knowing this first, that there shall come in the last days scoffers, walking after their own lusts,* **4** *And saying, Where is the promise of his coming? for since the fathers fell asleep, all things continue as they were from the beginning of the creation.*

It had been so very long since they had seen him, they reasoned that he was never coming back, and thus their surprise. Even though he had told them that they would bow before him, they were still surprised to see him.

Jesus ascended back into Heaven nearly two thousand years ago, but not before He explicitly gave us the promise that He would return.

John 14:1 *Let not your heart be troubled: ye believe in God, believe also in me.* **2** *In my Father's house are many mansions: if it were not so, I would have told you. I go to prepare a place for you.* **3** *And if I go and prepare a place for you, I will come again, and receive you unto myself; that where I am, there ye may be also.*

If a person is surprised at His coming, it is not because He did not tell them!

They had never been brought into account for any of their wrongdoing, and they figured they never would be. The lives and histories of the brothers of Joseph are sad tales of deeds gone unpunished. They were allowed to continue unabated and uncorrected in their wrongdoing. Judah committed fornication and incest yet incurred no punishment. Simeon and Levi murdered an entire city of helpless men, and no judgment was leveled upon them. Reuben slept with Bilhah, his father's concubine, his father heard of it, and yet nothing was done. When children are thus taught that their evil deeds will not be recompensed, they will be all the more emboldened in and encouraged in their wickedness. For all of their years, they were never brought into account for any of their wrongdoing, and that made their surprise all the more intense to find themselves standing before Joseph to face their wrongs.

They still remembered Joseph as the "sacrificial lamb" and did not recognize him as the all powerful judge. The brothers of Joseph remembered him and knew him as the baby brother whom they had sacrificed for their own benefit. That Joseph they knew, oh, so well. But the Joseph standing before them, the all powerful judge holding their lives in his hands, that Joseph they did not recognize, thus making their surprise complete.

Once again, Joseph is shown as a picture of Christ Himself. The world knows Him and recognizes Him as the Sacrificial Lamb. Even those who refuse to accept Him know that He died for them. But there is coming a day in which He will reveal Himself in a new, frightening role for us:

Acts 17:31 *Because he hath appointed a day, in the which he will judge the world in righteousness by that man whom he hath ordained; whereof he hath given assurance unto all men, in that he hath raised him from the dead.*

Do you know the most frightening words these men ever heard? "I am Joseph." Do you know the most frightening words the rest of mankind will ever hear? "I am Jesus."

"You killed Me, but I am alive, I am Jesus. You buried Me, but I came out of the ground, I am Jesus. You forgot about Me because I was gone for so long, but ready or not here I am, I am Jesus. You didn't believe Me when I told you that every knee would bow before Me, but go ahead and bow the knee whether you like it or not, I am Jesus. You lived your life like I "was not," but I am, so it's time for you to answer to Me, I am Jesus. You had every chance to accept Me, but you rejected Me, depart from Me forever, I am Jesus..."

Chapter 16
Dispelling the Darkness

Genesis 45:4 *And Joseph said unto his brethren, Come near to me, I pray you. And they came near. And he said, I am Joseph your brother, whom ye sold into Egypt.* **5** *Now therefore be not grieved, nor angry with yourselves, that ye sold me hither: for God did send me before you to preserve life.* **6** *For these two years hath the famine been in the land: and yet there are five years, in the which there shall neither be earing nor harvest.* **7** *And God sent me before you to preserve you a posterity in the earth, and to save your lives by a great deliverance.* **8** *So now it was not you that sent me hither, but God: and he hath made me a father to Pharaoh, and lord of all his house, and a ruler throughout all the land of Egypt.* **9** *Haste ye, and go up to my father, and say unto him, Thus saith thy son Joseph, God hath made me lord of all Egypt: come down unto me, tarry not:* **10** *And thou shalt dwell in the land of Goshen, and thou shalt be near unto me, thou, and thy children, and thy children's children, and thy flocks, and thy herds, and all that thou hast:* **11** *And there will I nourish thee; for yet there are five years of famine; lest thou, and thy household, and all that thou hast, come to poverty.* **12** *And, behold, your eyes see, and the eyes of my brother Benjamin, that it is my mouth that speaketh unto you.* **13** *And ye shall tell my father of all my glory in Egypt, and of all that ye have seen; and ye shall haste and bring down my father hither.* **14** *And he fell upon his brother Benjamin's neck, and wept; and Benjamin wept upon his neck.* **15** *Moreover* *he kissed all his brethren, and wept upon them: and after that his brethren talked with him.*

For Joseph, the storm washed over him many years earlier in a flash, sweeping him away into a foreign land. But the sun would eventually shine again, and he carried on with life. For his brothers, the sun shined the day they sold Joseph into slavery, but the clouds began to gather shortly thereafter. The darkness reached its peak when they found themselves standing before their brother, whom they had presumed to be dead or at least absent forever. Suddenly, they found themselves helpless, hopeless, and terrified. Things were as dark as they could possibly be.

A Reminder

Genesis 45:4 *And Joseph said unto his brethren, Come near to me, I pray you. And they came near. And he said, I am Joseph your brother, whom ye sold into Egypt.*

Truly making things right is only impeded by refusing to acknowledge wrongs done. This is true of the ones guilty of the wrong, and also of the ones to whom the wrong has been done. Joseph, in beginning the process of having things made right, began by reminding his brothers of what they had done. He said, "I am Joseph your brother, whom ye sold into Egypt." This served a dual purpose. It removed all possibility of fraud or trickery from the equation. These men had told no one of their foul deed, they had buried it, and removed it from remembrance. For this person standing before them to name the name of Joseph, whose name they had never uttered in his presence, and then recount their selling him into Egypt, proved beyond doubt that he was in fact Joseph.

But it also took everyone right back to where they had left off all of those years earlier. It took them back to the time when they should have apologized, lifted him from the pit, and repented. That is exactly where they needed to be brought back to for their own benefit. They needed to repent for what they had done, and that would require their being reminded of what they had done.

A Redirection

Genesis 45:5 *Now therefore be not grieved, nor angry with yourselves, that ye sold me hither: for God did send me before you to preserve life.*

Once and yet again, Joseph demonstrates himself to be a remarkable picture of Christ. His brothers stand before him guilty of betrayal and what they believed had been his death. But he, looking upon them, tells them not to be grieved or angry with themselves because God was the ultimate authority behind what they did. God used all of what his brothers did to save their lives, and indeed, the lives of the whole world, upon whom the famine had come.

Our world, too, was in a famine, wasting away towards death. It was a result of our own wicked sin, culminating in mankind's betrayal and crucifixion of Jesus Christ. None of this caught God by surprise. In fact, in ways that are too deep to fully fathom, God Himself was behind it all from the very beginning:

Revelation 13:8 *And all that dwell upon the earth shall worship him, whose names are not written in the book of life of the Lamb slain **from the foundation of the world.***

Before there was an Adam, a serpent, or a sin, there was a plan for the sacrificial death of Christ upon Calvary. God the Father chose it and was even pleased by it:

Isaiah 53:10 *Yet it pleased the LORD to bruise him; he hath put **him** to grief: when thou shalt make **his** soul an offering for sin, he shall see **his** seed, he shall prolong his days, and the pleasure of the LORD shall prosper in his hand.*

The brothers of Joseph sinned grievously when they betrayed him and sold him into slavery. Yet God was pleased by it, knew of it afore time, and ordained it to be the method of saving mankind from certain death. Mankind sinned grievously when we betrayed Jesus, sold Him out for the price of a slave and crucified the Lord of Glory. Yet God was pleased by it, knew of it afore time, and ordained it to be the method of saving mankind from death and Hell.

Genesis 45:6 *For these two years hath the famine been in the land: and yet there are five years, in the which there shall neither be earing nor harvest. 7 And God sent me before you to preserve you a posterity in the earth, and to save your lives by a* *great deliverance.* **8** *So now it was not you that sent me hither, but God: and he hath made me a father to Pharaoh, and lord of all his house, and a ruler throughout all the land of Egypt.*

After revealing the generalities of the plan of God in all that had transpired, Joseph began to unveil the specifics. There had been two years of famine. That, the brothers knew. But what they did not know is that "this dreamer" as they had once so derisively called him, had a revelation from God, through a dream, of how long the famine would last, and how bad it would be. Two years had past, he told them, but five more were yet to come. It was for that reason that God had sent him into Egypt, and brought him into the very household of Pharaoh as a ruler throughout Egypt.

Genesis 45:9 *Haste ye, and go up to my father, and say unto him, Thus saith thy son Joseph, God hath made me lord of all Egypt: come down unto me, tarry not:*

The command of Joseph in this verse had the marks of death and judgement upon it once again for his brothers. How could they go home and tell their father what Joseph just commanded them to tell him without admitting to what they had done? What was to stop the father from demanding their death? Simply this, the son, Joseph, was interested in their life, not their death! Likewise, the only thing that keeps the Father from demanding our death is that the Son, Jesus, has given us life!

Genesis 45:10 *And thou shalt dwell in the land of Goshen, and thou shalt be near unto me, thou, and thy children, and thy children's children, and thy flocks, and thy herds, and all that thou hast:* **11** *And there will I nourish thee; for yet there are five years of famine; lest thou, and thy household, and all that thou hast, come to poverty.*

Many years previous, Joseph had lain in a pit, while his brothers ate their meal above him. Now, when the fortunes of all had been diametrically reversed, Joseph chose to nourish the brothers who had starved him, and also to nourish their entire families and all of their flocks. Oh great mercy, that the betrayed son would thus nourish those that so wronged him, and that the betrayed Son would thus nourish those that so wronged Him!

Genesis 45:12 *And, behold, your eyes see, and the eyes of my brother Benjamin, that it is my mouth that speaketh unto* *you.* **13** *And ye shall tell my father of all my glory in Egypt, and of all that ye have seen; and ye shall haste and bring down my father hither.*

No longer speaking by an interpreter, Joseph now appeals to his brothers to recognize his mouth, his speech, his dialect; to think back to their youth and to his and to know him for who he is.

He then, still in command of his elders, commands that they tell his father of all of his glory and bring him down into Egypt. He may still be their younger brother, but he is also still in charge of either taking their lives or sparing them. May we never get so familiar with Jesus as our Brother that we fail to recognize Him as our Lord and Master!

A Reunion
Genesis 45:14 *And he fell upon his brother Benjamin's neck, and wept; and Benjamin wept upon his neck.* **15** *Moreover he kissed all his brethren, and wept upon them: and after that his brethren talked with him.*

The sequence of events is telling. Joseph first fell on Benjamin's neck and wept, and his baby brother Benjamin reciprocated. It is logical for this to take place first. He then kissed all of his brethren; every last one of them that had so cruelly taken from him all of the dearest things of earth. It is equally logical for this to take place second. It was then, and only then, that his brothers talked to him. It took a show of true affection from the betrayed son for the betrayers to believe that He was not going to harm them, and that, indeed, he loved them! And so with tears, hugs, and forgiveness the darkness was dispelled.

Chapter 17
Just the Son

Genesis 45:16 *And the fame thereof was heard in Pharaoh's house, saying, Joseph's brethren are come: and it pleased Pharaoh well, and his servants.* **17** *And Pharaoh said unto Joseph, Say unto thy brethren, This do ye; lade your beasts, and go, get you unto the land of Canaan;* **18** *And take your father and your households, and come unto me: and I will give you the good of the land of Egypt, and ye shall eat the fat of the land.* **19** *Now thou art commanded, this do ye; take you wagons out of the land of Egypt for your little ones, and for your wives, and bring your father, and come.* **20** *Also regard not your stuff; for the good of all the land of Egypt is yours.* **21** *And the children of Israel did so: and Joseph gave them wagons, according to the commandment of Pharaoh, and gave them provision for the way.* **22** *To all of them he gave each man changes of raiment; but to Benjamin he gave three hundred pieces of silver, and five changes of raiment.* **23** *And to his father he sent after this manner; ten asses laden with the good things of Egypt, and ten she asses laden with corn and bread and meat for his father by the way.* **24** *So he sent his brethren away, and they departed: and he said unto them, See that ye fall not out by the way.* **25** *And they went up out of Egypt, and came into the land of Canaan unto Jacob their father,* **26** *And told him, saying, Joseph is yet alive, and he is governor over all the land of Egypt. And Jacob's heart fainted, for he believed them not.* **27** *And they told him all the words of Joseph, which he had* *said unto them: and when he saw the wagons which Joseph had sent to carry him, the spirit of Jacob their father revived:* **28** *And Israel said, It is enough; Joseph my son is yet alive: I will go and see him before I die.*

    For some twenty years, Jacob, the son of Isaac, the son of Abraham, had been in mourning over his son, Joseph. No sunrise ever cheered him; no night of sleep ever comforted him. Food held no interest to him, pleasure no allure; life without the son was one worthless day after another.

    But then a famine brought the brothers of Joseph into Egypt to buy food. In the last two chapters we saw how Joseph finally revealed himself to them, and reassured them that they were safe in his presence. But Jacob had no way of knowing any of this. He was still back home in Canaan, scared to death that he was going to lose Benjamin as well.

    When the sons finally came home, carrying all of the treasures that Joseph sent, look once more at how Jacob responded in verse 28:

    Genesis 45:28 *And Israel said, It is enough; Joseph my son is yet alive: I will go and see him before I die.*

    Not, "It is enough; the food will keep us from starving." Not, "It is enough, ten asses laded down with treasure." Not, "It is enough; we are moving to a better place." No, the only thing that mattered to Jacob was that Joseph was alive, and he was going to see him.

A Coat-Tail Reputation

    Right after Joseph's tearful, noisy reunion with his brothers, we read this:

    Genesis 45:16 *And the fame thereof was heard in Pharaoh's house, saying, Joseph's brethren are come: and it pleased Pharaoh well, and his servants.*

    Why should it please Pharaoh? Why should it please him that murderers like Simeon and Levi were there? Why should it please him that an incestuous whoremonger like Judah was there? Why should it please him that a weak and whining man like Reuben, a man so "unstable" that he slept with his own father's wife, was there? Why should it please him that the men who thought so little of Joseph as to sell him into slavery was there? Why? Because he did not know them, or their character, but he did know Joseph and his character! Pharaoh thinks well of them because he thinks well of Joseph. Pharaoh and his servants are "well pleased" because they figure the family of Joseph will be just as big of a blessing as Joseph has been.

Who is Joseph a type of? Christ.

Who is the family of Christ? We are.

Pharaoh should have been able to expect the family of Joseph to be like Joseph. The world should be able to expect that the family of Christ will be like Christ. When we label ourselves as Christians, it is a weighty responsibility. He did everything necessary to give Himself and His family an excellent reputation. If you call yourself a Christian and then behave badly, you are destroying the reputation that Christ worked so hard to build for you. Look down through these next few verses with me, and you will see just how much Pharaoh thought of Joseph.

Genesis 45:17 *And Pharaoh said unto Joseph, Say unto thy brethren, This do ye; lade your beasts, and go, get you unto the land of Canaan;* **18** *And take your father and your households, and come unto me: and I will give you the good of the land of Egypt, and ye shall eat the fat of the land.*

Notice first of all that Pharaoh extended this offer to Joseph's brothers, his father, and all of their wives, children, and grandchildren, without even knowing how many of them there were or what character they possessed.

The second thing to notice is that Pharaoh said, "I won't just help them survive, I'll give them the best that Egypt has to offer." Then notice that Pharaoh himself arranged their transportation. Verse 19 says that he sent some wagons after them from Egypt. He did not know them, yet he told them to come, gave them of the fat of the land, and arranged and provided for their transportation.

Genesis 45:20 *Also regard not your stuff; for the good of all the land of Egypt is yours.*

This is quite honestly a bit arrogant on Pharaoh's part: "Don't bring your stuff, leave it behind, and we'll give you good stuff when you get here!" But it still goes to show how excellent a reputation this family had due to Joseph. Pharaoh told total strangers, "Come live with me, I'll treat you like royalty. I'll come pick you up to bring you here, and you don't even have to pack a suitcase, because I'll give you all new stuff when you get here."

Why in the world would Pharaoh do all of this for foreigners, total strangers? One word: Joseph. They had an excellent reputation because of the life and character of Joseph.

A Concerned Regulation

Genesis 45:21 *And the children of Israel did so: and Joseph gave them wagons, according to the commandment of Pharaoh, and gave them provision for the way.*

After getting the command from Pharaoh, Joseph began to implement it. He procured the wagons, a bunch of them, and got them ready to roll. He also "gave them provision for the way." He loaded them down with food for the journey. But the next two verses are where things get interesting:

Genesis 45:22 *To all of them he gave each man changes of raiment; but to Benjamin he gave three hundred pieces of silver, and five changes of raiment.* **23** *And to his father he sent after this manner; ten asses laden with the good things of Egypt, and ten she asses laden with corn and bread and meat for his father by the way.*

Now I want you to think back to these men's past. What had their problem always been? Jealousy. Now here is Joseph sending them home to get dad and their families. And out of the kindness of his heart, he gives them all a change of clothes. So far, things are good. But then, Joseph gives his little brother, Benjamin, not one, but five new sets of clothes! And, and, AND, three hundred pieces of silver! And instantly, the big green monster, jealousy, begins to set in. How do I know? Look at the very next verse:

Genesis 45:24 *So he sent his brethren away, and they departed: and he said unto them, See that ye fall not out by the way.*

This verse means exactly what it sounds like: see that you don't have a falling out on the way home. He said that right after he gave them these gifts! They had already sold him into slavery because he had a beautiful coat that they did not have, and now he is sending them on a long journey with his baby brother, who has just been given five sets of clothes to their one and 300 pieces of silver in addition to that. No wonder he said, "See that ye fall not out by the way!"

We would do well to stop for a moment and look at this, because this is right down where we live. People are really bad about being blessed yet getting jealous because others get blessed more.

Stop and think of these men and this situation. You may be tempted to say, "Well Joseph should have treated them all the same!" What gives you that idea? Let me ask you a question: did Joseph or did he not give them more than what they had when they got there? Yes. Didn't Joseph give them more than what they deserved? Yes. If they had been completely unaware of the fact that Joseph gave more to Benjamin, wouldn't they have been perfectly happy with what he gave them? Yes. So did they have any right whatsoever to be envious, especially considering that what they really deserved was to be put to death? No! Man's jealousy is always wicked and never warranted. People should be taught from their youth to be happy for what they receive and be happy for others when they receive even more. No where does God command that all be treated equally at all times! Only three were allowed to be with Him on the Mount of Transfiguration. Only one walked on water with him. Only one was allowed to live a long life.

The brothers of Joseph came into Egypt worthy of nothing but death. Anything good that they received is more than they were worthy of, and thus, they had no right at all to be jealous when Benjamin received more than they did.

Proverbs 14:30 *A sound heart is the life of the flesh: but envy the rottenness of the bones.*

Proverbs 27:4 *Wrath is cruel, and anger is outrageous; but who is able to stand before envy?*

This is a typical thing with children. I am still teaching mine out of it. If one gets to go on a trip, the others are upset that they didn't get to go. If one gets to sing, the others are mad that they didn't get to. Over and over we tell these kids, who will one day be adults, jealousy is wicked. Be happy for others when something good happens for them.

Parents, maybe you've outgrown your own jealousy and now get jealous on behalf of your children. That is still just as wicked! If little Bobby down the street gets into the starting lineup and your little Joey rides the bench, don't be jealous, and teach little Joey not to be jealous either. If little Susie gets to sing and little Bertha doesn't, don't be jealous, and teach little Bertha to be happy for little Susie. God has been good to every single one of us and every single one of our children. He has given us all "a change of raiment" that we do not deserve. Jealousy ruins friendships, hurts churches, and causes ulcers.

But maybe you still aren't convinced. Maybe deep down you still don't think you should be happy when others are blessed. Let me show you one passage of Scripture that all by itself should just obliterate that idea.

Matthew 20:1 *For the kingdom of heaven is like unto a man that is an householder, which went out early in the morning to hire labourers into his vineyard.* **2** *And when he had agreed with the labourers for a penny a day, he sent them into his vineyard.* **3** *And he went out about the third hour, and saw others standing idle in the marketplace,* **4** *And said unto them; Go ye also into the vineyard, and whatsoever is right I will give you. And they went their way.* **5** *Again he went out about the sixth and ninth hour, and did likewise.* **6** *And about the eleventh hour he went out, and found others standing idle, and saith unto them, Why stand ye here all the day idle?* **7** *They say unto him, Because no man hath hired us. He saith unto them, Go ye also into the vineyard; and whatsoever is right, that shall ye receive.* **8** *So when even was come, the lord of the vineyard saith unto his steward, Call the labourers, and give them their hire, beginning from the last unto the first.* **9** *And when they came that were hired about the eleventh hour, they received every man a penny.* **10** *But when the first came, they supposed that they should have received more; and they likewise received every man a penny.* **11** *And when they had received it, they murmured against the goodman of the house,* **12** *Saying, These last have wrought but one hour, and thou hast made them equal unto us, which have borne the burden and heat of the day.* **13** *But he answered one of them, and said, Friend, I do thee no wrong: didst not thou agree with me for a penny?* **14** *Take that thine is, and go thy way: I will give unto this last, even as unto thee.* **15** *Is it not lawful for me to do what I will with mine own? Is thine eye evil, because I am good?*

Did you get that? Some worked all day and earned a penny. That is an eighth of a penny per hour. Some worked for only an hour and earned a penny. That is eight times more per hour than the others. And how did the workers respond? They got jealous. **Even though they got paid exactly what they agreed to, they got jealous**. And what did Christ say to them? Your eye is evil because I am good! I've done a nice thing for these people, and you are upset about it!

See that ye fall not out by the way! Never, never, never be jealous.

For many years Sir Walter Scott was the leading literary figure in the British Empire. No one could write as well as he. Then the works of Lord Byron began to appear, and their greatness was immediately evident. Soon an anonymous critic praised his poems in a letter to a London Paper. He declared that in the presence of these brilliant works of poetic genius, Sir Walter Scott could no longer be considered the leading poet of England. Do you think that Sir Walter Scott was a little bit jealous? No. He was the one who wrote the letter! [2]

Never, never, never be jealous!

A Complete Restoration

Genesis 45:25 *And they went up out of Egypt, and came into the land of Canaan unto Jacob their father,* **26** *And told him, saying, Joseph is yet alive, and he is governor over all the land of Egypt. And Jacob's heart fainted, for he believed them not.*

Now, let's really get our minds into the mind of Jacob for just a moment. Let me describe it for you, so you can somewhat grasp what he felt.

For months, Jacob has been worried sick. Simeon has been in prison in Egypt and now Benjamin is gone and Jacob just knows he's going to lose him too. All that is in addition to spending the last twenty-plus years mourning for Joseph.

The house has been so quite since all twelve of the boys have been gone for the last few months. No doubt Jacob has even begun to fear that all of his children are now trapped in Egypt forever and that he will never see any of them again. Then one day there is a little dust cloud off on the horizon. The cloud gets bigger and bigger, and finally Jacob realizes that it is an enormous caravan. His heart must have just sunk with fear, wondering what it meant.

He would of course have gone out to meet the caravan; that was just the way of people in the Middle East. As he did, wondering what strangers were about to step down into his yard, he had to have gasped as he saw Reuben step down. And then Simeon, and Levi, and Judah, and all the way down the list, until finally his precious Benjamin appeared.

But what could be the meaning of the wagons, and the twenty donkeys loaded with treasure? Something big was happening. He was going to demand an immediate explanation, so they had to come out with it. "Dad, all of this stuff is from... it's, it's, from Joseph. Dad he's alive, and he's in charge of all Egypt. Dad, Joseph is alive, he's the man who imprisoned Simeon and made us bring Benjamin, Dad, and he sent all this. Joseph is alive..."

Jacob nearly died just from hearing that. In fact, he wanted to believe them, but couldn't, so the old man's heart just fainted, stopped beating for a few seconds.

Genesis 45:27 *And they told him all the words of Joseph, which he had said unto them: and when he saw the wagons which Joseph had sent to carry him, the spirit of Jacob their father revived:* **28** *And Israel said, It is enough; Joseph my son is yet alive: I will go and see him before I die.*

It wasn't the bags of corn that revived Jacob, it was just the son. It wasn't the gold and silver that revived Jacob, it was just the son. It wasn't the wagons that revived Jacob, it was just the son. It wasn't the new clothes that revived Jacob, it was just the son. The son was all he wanted. Without the son, even the good things in life were meaningless.

Who is it that saw the need of fallen man, and instituted the shedding of substitutionary blood? It was just the Son!

Who was it that left Heaven above, wrapped Himself in flesh, and came to Earth? It was just the Son!

Who was it that spent thirty-three years living a life of rejection so that you and I could be accepted? It was just the Son!

Who was it that sweat great drops of blood in Gethsemane's garden? It was just the Son!

Who was it that carried a cross up Calvary's hill, hung between Heaven and Earth, and shed His precious blood? It was just the Son!

Who was it that the Father couldn't wait to see just three days later, coming home victorious over death and the grave? It was just the Son!

Who is it that has been saving souls and building His church for two thousand years now? It is just the Son!

Who is it that fixes broken homes, cures diseased bodies, takes the taste of liquor out of a drunk's mouth, makes an honest man out of a liar, cleanses a harlot like the wind driven snow? It's just the Son!

Who is it that makes every day seem bright, gives you a reason for living, and makes sure you never have to spend a second in Hell? It's just the Son! It's just the Son! It's just the Son!

Chapter 18
A Reunion for the Ages

Genesis 46:1 *And Israel took his journey with all that he had, and came to Beersheba, and offered sacrifices unto the God of his father Isaac.* **2** *And God spake unto Israel in the visions of the night, and said, Jacob, Jacob. And he said, Here am I.* **3** *And he said, I am God, the God of thy father: fear not to go down into Egypt; for I will there make of thee a great nation:* **4** *I will go down with thee into Egypt; and I will also surely bring thee up again: and Joseph shall put his hand upon thine eyes.* **5** *And Jacob rose up from Beersheba: and the sons of Israel carried Jacob their father, and their little ones, and their wives, in the wagons which Pharaoh had sent to carry him.* **6** *And they took their cattle, and their goods, which they had gotten in the land of Canaan, and came into Egypt, Jacob, and all his seed with him:* **7** *His sons, and his sons' sons with him, his daughters, and his sons' daughters, and all his seed brought he with him into Egypt.* **8** *And these are the names of the children of Israel, which came into Egypt, Jacob and his sons: Reuben, Jacob's firstborn.* **9** *And the sons of Reuben; Hanoch, and Phallu, and Hezron, and Carmi.* **10** *And the sons of Simeon; Jemuel, and Jamin, and Ohad, and Jachin, and Zohar, and Shaul the son of a Canaanitish woman.* **11** *And the sons of Levi; Gershon, Kohath, and Merari.* **12** *And the sons of Judah; Er, and Onan, and Shelah, and Pharez, and Zerah: but Er and Onan died in the land of Canaan. And the sons of Pharez were Hezron and Hamul.* **13** *And the sons of Issachar; Tola, and*

Phuvah, and Job, and Shimron. **14** *And the sons of Zebulun; Sered, and Elon, and Jahleel.* **15** *These be the sons of Leah, which she bare unto Jacob in Padanaram, with his daughter Dinah: all the souls of his sons and his daughters were thirty and three.* **16** *And the sons of Gad; Ziphion, and Haggi, Shuni, and Ezbon, Eri, and Arodi, and Areli.* **17** *And the sons of Asher; Jimnah, and Ishuah, and Isui, and Beriah, and Serah their sister: and the sons of Beriah; Heber, and Malchiel.* **18** *These are the sons of Zilpah, whom Laban gave to Leah his daughter, and these she bare unto Jacob, even sixteen souls.* **19** *The sons of Rachel Jacob's wife; Joseph, and Benjamin.* **20** *And unto Joseph in the land of Egypt were born Manasseh and Ephraim, which Asenath the daughter of Potipherah priest of On bare unto him.* **21** *And the sons of Benjamin were Belah, and Becher, and Ashbel, Gera, and Naaman, Ehi, and Rosh, Muppim, and Huppim, and Ard.* **22** *These are the sons of Rachel, which were born to Jacob: all the souls were fourteen.* **23** *And the sons of Dan; Hushim.* **24** *And the sons of Naphtali; Jahzeel, and Guni, and Jezer, and Shillem.* **25** *These are the sons of Bilhah, which Laban gave unto Rachel his daughter, and she bare these unto Jacob: all the souls were seven.* **26** *All the souls that came with Jacob into Egypt, which came out of his loins, besides Jacob's sons' wives, all the souls were threescore and six;* **27** *And the sons of Joseph, which were born him in Egypt, were two souls: all the souls of the house of Jacob, which came into Egypt, were threescore and ten.* **28** *And he sent Judah before him unto Joseph, to direct his face unto Goshen; and they came into the land of Goshen.* **29** *And Joseph made ready his chariot, and went up to meet Israel his father, to Goshen, and presented himself unto him; and he fell on his neck, and wept on his neck a good while.* **30** *And Israel said unto Joseph, Now let me die, since I have seen thy face, because thou art yet alive.*

Daytime talk shows are always looking for incredible stories of reunions. Twins separated at birth, who found each other by accident after forty years. High school sweethearts who went different ways, and then reunited and got married in their sixties. Everyone loves stories like that.

Well friends, imagine the ratings you would get with a promo like this one:

"On the next Maury Ellen De Banks show, a tearful reunion between an old man and his son. This boy was kidnapped by his own brothers, sold into slavery, taken to a foreign country, thrown into prison for a crime he didn't commit, but somehow ended up as governor over that entire country. Be here with us next week when father and son see each other for the first time in more than twenty years, and we'll even give you a chance to talk to the dead-beat brothers who did him so wrong."

Everyone in America would be tuning in; that would truly be a reunion for the ages!

The Fear of Jacob
Genesis 46:1 *And Israel took his journey with all that he had, and came to Beersheba, and offered sacrifices unto the God of his father Isaac.*

Jacob and his family at this time lived in Hebron. After getting everything ready, the entire family traveled twenty-five miles southwest and came to the southern edge of the Promised Land. They stopped at a place that was very special to them, a place named Beersheba. It was special for several reasons. First of all, when you left Beersheba, it was not many more steps till you were out of Canaan altogether. So this would be like leaving America and stopping for a minute right at the border to look back.

But this place also had special personal meaning to Jacob. God had met with his grandfather, Abraham, in Beersheba in Genesis 21. And then the same thing happened to his father Isaac in Genesis 26.

It is very clear then what Jacob had in mind. Something very big was happening, and he didn't want it to happen unless he met with God first. He learned that from his dad, he learned that from his granddad.

I wonder if dads and grandfathers today are teaching the same thing by their example that Abraham and Isaac taught by theirs.

I wonder if people today understand how important it is to meet with God, especially before some major event?

Genesis 46:2 *And God spake unto Israel in the visions of the night, and said, Jacob, Jacob. And he said, Here am I.* **3a** *And he said, I am God, the God of thy father...*

When you desire to meet with God, you will be pleasantly surprised to find out that God desires to meet with you. God met with Jacob, called him by name, and then introduced Himself as "the God of thy father."

Parents, how great will it be if your kids, when they are adults, can truly think of God as "the God of my mother, the God of my father." I wonder, do your kids see God like that? If you have a prayer life, don't keep it hidden from your kids. If you have a Bible reading life, don't keep it hidden from your kids. If you love and reverence God, don't keep it hidden from your kids. Devotion to God is caught, not taught! Let your kids catch that devotion from you.

Genesis 46:3 *And he said, I am God, the God of thy father: fear not to go down into Egypt; for I will there make of thee a great nation:*

Why was Jacob afraid to go down into Egypt? Joseph was down there, his favorite son that he had been longing for, for twenty some years. Yet he is still afraid to go down into Egypt. Why?

The past is the key to the present. In Genesis 26, God had forbidden his father Isaac from going into Egypt. In Genesis 12, he knew that God had promised Abraham and his descendants the land of Canaan, not the land of Egypt. But I believe the reason that was front and center in his mind was the specific words of a prophecy that God gave Abraham back in Genesis 15:13:

Genesis 15:13 *And he said unto Abram, Know of a surety that thy seed shall be a stranger in a land that is not theirs, and shall serve them; and they shall afflict them four hundred years;*

Joseph sends word, "Dad, come to me right away in Egypt!" So Jacob immediately packs up and starts that way.

But somewhere down the road, it dawns on him that God has already said that one day the family of Abraham would be afflicted and made slaves in Egypt! That memory must have hit him like a ton of bricks. So Jacob, in effect, pulls off to the side of the road and says, "Wait just a minute. I need to get ahold of God and make sure we're going to be ok if we actually go through with this."

Once again, what a great lesson to learn! Before you do anything, especially anything major, you better get in touch with God and make sure He is directing it. If He isn't, you're begging for trouble!

Jacob went to God for answers and for comfort, and God gave him both in the next verse when He said:

Genesis 46:4 *I will go down with thee into Egypt; and I will also surely bring thee up again: and Joseph shall put his hand upon thine eyes.*

God said the first thing Jacob needed to hear, "I will go down with you into Egypt." Jacob needed to hear that. He was scared to death that God was going to stop at the border of Canaan and stay right there while Jacob had to go on without Him. Jacob was saying, "God, if you aren't going, Joseph or not, I'm not going either." But that wasn't all that Jacob needed to hear. The fact that God was going with him into Egypt was wonderful, but Jacob also wanted to make sure that it wasn't a one-way trip. Jacob was saying, "God, I'm glad you're going with me, but I'm not going until you assure me that I'll be able to come back here."

Jacob was 130 years old at the time. He knew that what he was asking would only be fulfilled after he died. You can find that at the end of Genesis 47. That was fine with Jacob. Whether in life or death, though, he was determined to make it back to Canaan. Egypt was nicer, more modern, more comfortable. But Egypt wasn't home, Canaan was. Egypt wasn't the Promised Land, Canaan was.

Nothing the world can offer us can even hold a candle to the inheritance God has in store for us. We are in our Egypt right now. "This world is not my home, I'm only passing through, my treasures are laid up, somewhere beyond the blue, the angels beckon me from Heaven's open door, and I can't feel at home in this world anymore."

The great fear of Jacob was not getting back home. God let Jacob know that He would bring him home. He has given us the same assurance:

John 14:1 *Let not your heart be troubled: ye believe in God, believe also in me.* **2** *In my Father's house are many mansions: if it were not so, I would have told you. I go to prepare a place for you.* **3** *And if I go and prepare a place for you, I will come again, and receive you unto myself; that where I am, there ye may be also.*

1 Thessalonians 4:16 *For the Lord himself shall descend from heaven with a shout, with the voice of the archangel, and with the trump of God: and the dead in Christ shall rise first:* **17** *Then we which are alive and remain shall be caught up together with them in the clouds, to meet the Lord in the air: and so shall we ever be with the Lord.* **18** *Wherefore comfort one another with these words.*

God may have us suffering in Egypt for the present, but dear child of God, one day we are going Home.

The Fondness of Canaan

This thought ties in with the previous one in a very unique way. Look at these verses with me, and let me show you something:

Genesis 46:5 *And Jacob rose up from Beersheba: and the sons of Israel carried Jacob their father, and their little ones, and their wives, in the wagons which Pharaoh had sent to carry him.* **6** *And they took their cattle, and their goods, which they had gotten in the land of Canaan, and came into Egypt, Jacob, and all his seed with him:*

Do you remember what instruction Pharaoh gave them concerning their stuff?

Genesis 45:20 *Also regard not your stuff; for the good of all the land of Egypt is yours.*

Pharaoh said, "Leave all the stuff from Canaan behind. When you get here, I'll give you good stuff. Jacob intentionally disregarded that. He had been told to leave his stuff behind, but he took it with him anyway. Why? If you have to be in Egypt instead of Canaan, you may as well carry as much Canaan into Egypt as you can. If you have to be on Earth instead of in

Heaven, you may as well carry as much Heaven on Earth as you can!

The Favorable Dwelling Place

Genesis 46:28 *And he sent Judah before him unto Joseph, to direct his face unto Goshen; and they came into the land of Goshen.*

I am constantly amazed at the providential care of God. He handles things in such amazing detail, and this is a beautiful example of it. Let me tell you a little bit about Goshen and why God and Joseph had them settle there.

Goshen was the nearest spot in Egypt to Canaan. Neither Joseph nor God wanted the Israelites to get too used to being in Egypt, and God wanted to make sure that four hundred years later when it came time for them to go, they would already be right there on the border, sitting right by the exit door. What an application that has for us today! God wants us to be living as near to the edges of this wicked old world as we can, not getting too comfortable here, so we will be ready to go in a moment, in the twinkling of an eye.

There also weren't many actual Egyptians living in the land of Goshen. So by placing the family there, they were far less likely to be assimilated into the culture and race of Egypt. They could remain a separate and distinct people there. And that plan worked beautifully! Four hundred years later, when the Jews numbered some two million people, they were still a completely distinct race, far different in every way from the Egyptians. Once again, there is a good point for us in that:

2 Corinthians 6:17 *Wherefore come out from among them, and be ye separate, saith the Lord, and touch not the unclean thing; and I will receive you,* **18** *And will be a Father unto you, and ye shall be my sons and daughters, saith the Lord Almighty.*

God does not intend for us to be absorbed into our culture; He expects us to be as different from the culture as night is from day.

Furthermore, in Goshen they could continue in the occupation that God had called them to do. Goshen was the best place in Egypt to be a shepherd. It was well watered, with good pasture land, and the Egyptians would not bother them there even though they despised shepherds.

Always let God place you where you can continue to serve Him. There was nothing glorious about being a shepherd, but that is what God wanted them to do. People tend to think only of money, but the truth is that doing what God wants you to do for $20,000 a year is a lot better than doing something He doesn't want you to do for $20,000,000 a year.

Goshen was indeed a favorable place for Israel to dwell!

The Father's Honor
Genesis 46:29 *And Joseph made ready his chariot, and went up to meet Israel his father, to Goshen, and presented himself unto him...*

Let me describe two men for you: man number one is young, healthy, filthy-rich, famous, the second most powerful man on earth. Man number two is old, decrepit, poor, unknown, and helplessly dependent on strangers for food. Which one is worthy of being honored?

Most would be tempted to say man number one, of course! But if you will pay attention to the verse we just read, man number one, the young, healthy, filthy-rich, famous, second most powerful man on Earth, left the palace, and went down personally to present himself to man number two. Joseph didn't have Jacob brought to him, he brought himself to Jacob down in Goshen. Why? Because Jacob was also daddy.

Young people, there is a high likelihood that you will one day become better off financially than your parents. You will most likely one day be still young and healthy while they are drooling on themselves. You may very well become famous while they fade into obscurity. But you listen to me, you would not be here without them, you would not have survived infancy if they had not fed you, changed you, tended to you, and taught you. No matter how far you go in life, honor thy father and thy mother!

The Family Reunion
Genesis 46:29 *And Joseph made ready his chariot, and went up to meet Israel his father, to Goshen, and presented himself unto him; and he fell on his neck, and wept on his neck*

a good while. **30** *And Israel said unto Joseph, Now let me die, since I have seen thy face, because thou art yet alive.*

More than twenty years before, Jacob had sent Joseph out to check on his brothers. Jacob watched Joseph walk out the door that morning, never dreaming it would be for, apparently, the last time. Think of what that was like. Parents can figure it out easily. Jacob replayed that day in his mind ten thousand times, day after day, year after year. He beat himself up, blamed himself for sending him, racked his brain thinking of whether he could have done anything to bring Joseph back safely. He went nights on end without sleep, sobbing through them till the sun rose on bleak, meaningless days. Joseph's back, clad in a many-colored coat, was the last he ever saw of him, walking out the door.

Twenty-some years later, the door opened again, this time in Goshen, and his precious baby-boy walked in again. In a split second of time, twenty years of grief came flooding out of them. But I am struck by the fact that the Bible specifically mentions that Joseph fell on Jacob's neck, and Joseph cried on his neck for a long time. It doesn't say that Jacob cried, it says that Joseph cried, sobbed like a baby, for a good while. Why?

May I offer you a conjecture on that? Joseph knew, based on the prophecy of his dreams, that he would see his father again. So he had cried for a while but then had gone on with living his life, waiting for God to fulfill His promise. Jacob thought Joseph was dead. He cried from the first day, till he just couldn't cry anymore, and then spent the next twenty years mourning.

Jacob got weaker, but Joseph got stronger. He had to. He had to endure the trial in Potiphar's house. He had to make it through a few years in prison. He had to step up and save the entire world from a famine. Jacob was allowed many years of weakness, but Joseph was not. He had no choice but to be strong whether he wanted to or not.

But now, after years of having to be strong, Joseph walks in and there is daddy. In a split second, he isn't vice president Joseph anymore; he is his daddy's baby boy, and for the first time in years he has a safe place to run to, a safe place to cry, cradled in his daddy's arms. No one ever gets too big for daddy's arms when they are hurting. Years of grief were erased in daddy's arms.

When Joseph finally calmed down, Jacob held him out, looked at him and said, "I can die now, I've seen you, you're still alive..."

Things are often very hard down here in this old world. We have to deal with financial troubles... we have to deal with bad news from the doctor... we have to stand for what's right while people call us names and say all kinds of nasty things... we have to go through tragedy, heartache, discouragement, and we have no choice but to do our best to be strong with God's help. But one day, we won't have to even try to be strong anymore. One day, we'll enter into the presence of the Father, and we'll just crawl up into His arms, and weep on His neck a good while. My, my, my, won't that be a reunion for the ages.

Chapter 19
Honeymoon in Egypt

Genesis 46:31 *And Joseph said unto his brethren, and unto his father's house, I will go up, and shew Pharaoh, and say unto him, My brethren, and my father's house, which were in the land of Canaan, are come unto me;* **32** *And the men are shepherds, for their trade hath been to feed cattle; and they have brought their flocks, and their herds, and all that they have.* **33** *And it shall come to pass, when Pharaoh shall call you, and shall say, What is your occupation?* **34** *That ye shall say, Thy servants' trade hath been about cattle from our youth even until now, both we, and also our fathers: that ye may dwell in the land of Goshen; for every shepherd is an abomination unto the Egyptians.*
Genesis 47:1 *Then Joseph came and told Pharaoh, and said, My father and my brethren, and their flocks, and their herds, and all that they have, are come out of the land of Canaan; and, behold, they are in the land of Goshen.* **2** *And he took some of his brethren, even five men, and presented them unto Pharaoh.* **3** *And Pharaoh said unto his brethren, What is your occupation? And they said unto Pharaoh, Thy servants are shepherds, both we, and also our fathers.* **4** *They said moreover unto Pharaoh, For to sojourn in the land are we come; for thy servants have no pasture for their flocks; for the famine is sore in the land of Canaan: now therefore, we pray thee, let thy servants dwell in the land of Goshen.* **5** *And Pharaoh spake unto Joseph, saying, Thy father and thy brethren are come unto thee:*

6 The land of Egypt is before thee; in the best of the land make thy father and brethren to dwell; in the land of Goshen let them dwell: and if thou knowest any men of activity among them, then make them rulers over my cattle. 7 And Joseph brought in Jacob his father, and set him before Pharaoh: and Jacob blessed Pharaoh. 8 And Pharaoh said unto Jacob, How old art thou? 9 And Jacob said unto Pharaoh, The days of the years of my pilgrimage are an hundred and thirty years: few and evil have the days of the years of my life been, and have not attained unto the days of the years of the life of my fathers in the days of their pilgrimage. 10 And Jacob blessed Pharaoh, and went out from before Pharaoh. 11 And Joseph placed his father and his brethren, and gave them a possession in the land of Egypt, in the best of the land, in the land of Rameses, as Pharaoh had commanded. 12 And Joseph nourished his father, and his brethren, and all his father's household, with bread, according to their families.

Here in the year A.D. 2010, we have the benefit of being able to look back at Biblical history and know how things turned out for Israel in Egypt. We know that they ended up as slaves and that Pharaoh tried to exterminate them. We know that Hebrew baby boys were thrown into the Nile River to be eaten by crocodiles or to drown.

But when Jacob took his family into Egypt, they did not know any of those details. They did have a prophecy though, given to Abraham by God, which let them know they would be in for trouble, affliction of some sort. They also knew that God intended for them to be there for a very long time, four hundred years, but after that, they would be able to come back to the Promised Land.

Joseph took all of that into account when he brought his family into Egypt. He knew that he would have a brief window of time to get his family set up in good conditions -- conditions that would help them to survive the hardships to come.

The Benefit of Low Estate

Genesis 46:31 *And Joseph said unto his brethren, and unto his father's house, I will go up, and shew Pharaoh, and say unto him, My brethren, and my father's house, which were in the land of Canaan, are come unto me; 32 And the men are* *shepherds, for their trade hath been to feed cattle; and they have brought their flocks, and their herds, and all that they have.* **33** *And it shall come to pass, when Pharaoh shall call you, and shall say, What is your occupation?* **34** *That ye shall say, Thy servants' trade hath been about cattle from our youth even until now, both we, and also our fathers: that ye may dwell in the land of Goshen; for every shepherd is an abomination unto the Egyptians.*

One thing in this passage ought to capture your attention immediately, twice Joseph and his family are going to mention to Pharaoh that they are shepherds, yet the end of verse 34 says every shepherd is an abomination to the Egyptians.

Stop and consider this. There is something about these men that, if it becomes known, will make them absolutely disgusting in the eyes of the Egyptians. Yet rather than trying to hide it, or even make it the last thing mentioned after all of their "good traits," it is the very first thing they mention, and they mention it twice!

This is just not the normal way that people behave. Take a guy and a girl being set up for the first time on a date by their friends. When those two meet each other, it never goes like this:

"Hi, I'm Steve, and I pick my nose... and every now and then I eat what I dig out!"

"Hi Steve, I'm Lulu, and I don't bathe unless I have to. I just squirt on fresh perfume every day, and the hair under my arms is long enough to weave an Indian blanket."

No, Sir, that never happens! People either hide the worst parts about them, or at the very least, they slip it in at the very end of a glorious list:

"Hi, I graduated with honors from MIT, I was valedictorian, ran track, I donate 20 hours a week to local charities, I drive a Masaratti, live by the country club, and I wet the bed at least three times a week. So how's the weather been where you live?"

You see what I mean? Yet Joseph and his brothers walked right in before Pharaoh and told him the one thing for which he would despise them the very most! They didn't do it by accident. Joseph knew going in, and told his brothers, exactly how Pharaoh and all the Egyptians would feel about it.

That being the case, you know that there was a method to his madness. Joseph knew exactly what he was doing.

So what was he doing? There were two obvious goals here. First, he didn't want Egypt getting too fond of them. When wicked people like you too much, you end up getting invited all sorts of places you shouldn't be going and getting opportunities to do all sorts of things you shouldn't be doing. By telling everyone right up front that they were shepherds, they would be on the outskirts of society from then on out.

This is not a bad thing! Do you realize that a real live Christian will be just as big an abomination to the world? If you really live for God, if you girls dress like Christian young ladies, if you guys dress like Christian young men, if you only listen to gospel music, if you never cuss or tell dirty jokes, if you keep your hands off of each other, if you never drink or smoke or do drugs or get tattoos or pierce yourselves up, if you memorize your Bible and can quote it at a moments notice, you are not likely to ever be invited to get yourself into any inappropriate situations!

So the first thing Joseph wanted to accomplish was to make sure Egypt didn't get too fond of them. The second thing Joseph wanted to accomplish was to make sure that they didn't get too fond of Egypt! If Joseph had not let Pharaoh know these men were shepherds, they would most likely have been given the opportunity to rise to prominence like Joseph had, just based on how well they already thought of Joseph. They could have become wealthy and powerful men, and if they had, they would never have left Egypt. Just think of how hard it was to get them to leave while they were beaten and afflicted as slaves! These people, when they finally got their freedom, were begging to go back into Egypt, the very place where their babies were being killed, the place where they were beaten and abused and oppressed. If God just barely got them out of there as afflicted slaves, how impossible would it have been for Him to ever get them to march away if they were princes and nobles!

There is a blessing in being people of low estate. There is a blessing in not getting too popular or well known. There is a blessing in not rising to the pinnacle of our society. When it comes time to go, we'll be ready. In fact, we'll spend our days looking for Christ to come, waiting for the trumpet to blow, desiring that call to come up hither!

All these men did was tell the truth about who and what they were. If you are a born-again child of God, and you will be open and honest about it, if you will stand out rather than fit in, the world will never become too fond of you, and you will never become too fond of the world.

The Behavior of a Careful Man

Genesis 47:1 *Then Joseph came and told Pharaoh, and said, My father and my brethren, and their flocks, and their herds, and all that they have, are come out of the land of Canaan; and, behold, they are in the land of Goshen.* **2** *And he took some of his brethren, even five men, and presented them unto Pharaoh.*

You no doubt know that Joseph had eleven brothers. You also have learned enough about Joseph to realize that he doesn't do anything carelessly. If he does something, there is a reason for it. In this case, Joseph hand-picked five out of his eleven brothers, and brought them to Pharaoh. He did this even before he brought his father in.

What was Joseph up to? The word for "presented" is not a casual word. It means that he brought them up and exhibited them before Pharaoh. These five became the representatives for the entire family. Remember that not only did Joseph have his eleven brothers in Egypt, but also his entire family of more than seventy people! So let's look at what facts we do know and what applications we can draw from it.

Fact number one, Joseph did not know most of his family. He knew his brothers, he may have known one or two of their wives, but he really did not know any of his nephews, nieces, cousins, etc. So the people that he brought before Pharaoh to represent the family were people that he knew.

There is a very good, practical thing to see here. If you are going to have people represent you, it should be those you know:

Proverbs 22:1 *A good name is rather to be chosen than great riches, and loving favour rather than silver and gold.*

If you have a business, you do not want brand new, untested employees representing your company in noticeable positions; you want tried and true ones doing that. Same thing in a church. A church that has any sense does not offer people positions to get them to come; it gives positions to those who have been tried, tested, and faithful already.

A man from our church got off into sin several years back, and when we confronted him he left. A man from a church just a few miles away found out that he was not here anymore, searched him out, and offered to make him a Sunday school teacher if he would come there! He didn't even know what the man was involved in. That is being very careless.

Fact number two, Joseph did know all of his brothers, but he did not bring them all. He hand picked just a few to stand in for all the rest. There are two things you never want to do: you never want to have an unknown factor representing you, and you also never want to have a known, negative factor representing you. Joseph hand picked the ones that he thought would do the best standing before Pharaoh.

Once again, there are some great, practical things to say here. It is utterly foolish to have yourself represented by a known negative! This is why I tell our young people how I expect them to dress before they ever get into our youth choir, and our adults too for that matter. Anyone walking up onto our platform is a representative of our entire church. This is why before I have someone sing specials for us, or play instruments, I stop and consider how they live Monday through Saturday. I don't want a person cussing out there and singing in here. I don't want someone posting immodest pictures of him or herself on the internet and then helping in our youth programs. Is this being hard or mean? No, it's being careful, just like Joseph was.

The Building of an Understanding

Genesis 47:3 *And Pharaoh said unto his brethren, What is your occupation? And they said unto Pharaoh, Thy servants are shepherds, both we, and also our fathers.* **4** *They said moreover unto Pharaoh, For to sojourn in the land are we come; for thy servants have no pasture for their flocks; for the famine is sore in the land of Canaan: now therefore, we pray thee, let thy servants dwell in the land of Goshen.*

There is one word in this passage that is extremely important. It is the word *sojourn* found in verse 4. It means to stay somewhere temporarily, with the understanding that you are just passing through. Joseph was so very good at what he did. He built into everyone an understanding from the very beginning that Israel was not going to be in Egypt forever. No Pharaoh from that day forward had any excuse for failing to realize that Israel was leaving one day. No Israelite from that day forward had any excuse to think that Egypt was actually their home.

Most people don't seem to realize it anymore, but God has done the exact same thing for us, over and over again:

John 14:1 *Let not your heart be troubled: ye believe in God, believe also in me.* **2** *In my Father's house are many mansions: if it were not so, I would have told you. I go to prepare a place for you.* **3** *And if I go and prepare a place for you, I will come again, and receive you unto myself; that where I am, there ye may be also.*

1 Thessalonians 4:16 *For the Lord himself shall descend from heaven with a shout, with the voice of the archangel, and with the trump of God: and the dead in Christ shall rise first:* **17** *Then we which are alive and remain shall be caught up together with them in the clouds, to meet the Lord in the air: and so shall we ever be with the Lord.* **18** *Wherefore comfort one another with these words.*

1 Corinthians 15:50 *Now this I say, brethren, that flesh and blood cannot inherit the kingdom of God; neither doth corruption inherit incorruption.* **51** *Behold, I shew you a mystery; We shall not all sleep, but we shall all be changed,* **52** *In a moment, in the twinkling of an eye, at the last trump: for the trumpet shall sound, and the dead shall be raised incorruptible, and we shall be changed.*

Matthew 25:6 *And at midnight there was a cry made, Behold, the bridegroom cometh; go ye out to meet him.*

When the trumpet sounds for us, the world is going to be shocked, but with no good reason, because they have been told over and again that one day we're leaving!

When the trumpet sounds, many Christians are going to be absolutely unprepared, because they have gotten so used to this world, they thought they would be here forever. But there won't be any good reason for that, because God made it very plain that day is coming.

The Basis of an Opportunity

Genesis 47:5 *And Pharaoh spake unto Joseph, saying, Thy father and thy brethren are come unto thee:* **6** *The land of Egypt is before thee; in the best of the land make thy father and brethren to dwell; in the land of Goshen let them dwell: and if thou knowest any men of activity among them, then make them rulers over my cattle.*

There is no indication that either Joseph or his brothers knew that Pharaoh would say this. As far as we can tell, it was a wonderful, yet unexpected opportunity. Some of Joseph's brothers were going to get to be in charge of the flocks and herds of Pharaoh! Yet there was one basis for this opportunity -- if thou knowest any men of activity among them

That phrase "men of activity" means men who aren't lazy and idle, men who are strong, men who work long and hard.

This theme, that men ought to work hard, is ubiquitous in Scripture. Open your Bible to any page at random, and you won't have to do that very many times till you run across the subject in some way, shape, or form.

Pharaoh may have been a heathen, but he had a good head on his shoulders. Even lost people who are in any position of authority usually understand the benefit of finding hard workers!

When we were in the West Indies for a mission trip a few years ago, a gentleman got me hooked on this show about crab boats out in the Bering Sea. It is called *The Deadliest Catch*. From what I can tell, probably none of the captains on those boats are saved, but every one of them understands the value of a hard worker. Those men are amazing! They will be out at sea in fifteen foot waves, thirty below zero, beating tons of ice off the boat with big sledge hammers, then hauling in one thousand pound cages filled with giant crabs. They work thirty-six and forty-eight hours in row, then sleep for a few hours and do it again.

You who are employers, wouldn't you like to have somebody with that kind of work ethic? That is a "man of activity!"

This enormous opportunity, keeping Pharaoh's flocks, was given to them only on the basis of a solid work ethic, not on looks or age or talent.

There are many things I would like our young people to "catch" in our church while they are growing up, and one of them is a strong work ethic. I would like our guys and girls to be famous in these parts for how they work. I would like for employers all around here, when they find out someone is from Cornerstone to say, "Hire that one, I guarantee he or she will be a good worker!"

The Blessings of an Old Man
Genesis 47:7 *And Joseph brought in Jacob his father, and set him before Pharaoh: and Jacob blessed Pharaoh.*

Who was the ruler of the known world? Pharaoh. Who was the poor, wandering old man? Jacob. When Joseph brought in his brothers before Pharaoh, they were bowing, calling themselves his servants, asking for blessings from him. But when Jacob came in, he blessed Pharaoh! Let me show you how significant that was:

Hebrews 7:7 *And without all contradiction the less is blessed of the better.*

This is just striking. The brothers came in and said, "Pharaoh, we need your blessing." Jacob came in and said, "Pharaoh, you need my blessing." Hold that thought, we'll come back to it in just a minute, because in a couple of more verses, it happens again.

Genesis 47:8 *And Pharaoh said unto Jacob, How old art thou?*

Egypt was the most advanced civilization of its day. So much so that they had lots of luxury, processed foods, people to do their hard work for them, and tons of pollution. Little wonder then that they also had a very short life span! If you made it to age forty as an Egyptian, you were doing well. So when Jacob comes in before Pharaoh, you can almost hear the gasp from all the courtiers before Pharaoh finally asks how old are you? And look at the answer:

Genesis 47:9 *And Jacob said unto Pharaoh, The days of the years of my pilgrimage are an hundred and thirty years: few and evil have the days of the years of my life been, and have not attained unto the days of the years of the life of my fathers in the days of their pilgrimage.*

If Pharaoh was shocked by the appearance of a 130 year old man, the answer of that old man had to shock him even more: "I am 130, I've lived a short, evil life, I'm near death, and I'm not going to live near as long as my dad and granddad did."

He was telling the truth. He lived to be 147, but his daddy, Isaac, lived to be 180, and his granddaddy, Abraham, lived to be 175. Sin takes years off of your life! Jacob could have been a lot healthier, and lived a lot longer, if he hadn't been a conniving trickster who did everything his own way in his own power.

Genesis 47:10 *And Jacob blessed Pharaoh, and went out from before Pharaoh.*

This is the second time that Jacob has blessed Pharaoh, and there is something to it. For all of his flaws and sin, Jacob was no mere commoner. In fact, he was royalty. Many years before, at the brook Jabbok, Jacob had a little wrestling match with God:

Genesis 32:24 *And Jacob was left alone; and there wrestled a man with him until the breaking of the day.* **25** *And when he saw that he prevailed not against him, he touched the hollow of his thigh; and the hollow of Jacob's thigh was out of joint, as he wrestled with him.* **26** *And he said, Let me go, for the day breaketh. And he said, I will not let thee go, except thou bless me.* **27** *And he said unto him, What is thy name? And he said, Jacob.* **28** *And he said, Thy name shall be called no more Jacob, but Israel: for as a prince hast thou power with God and with men, and hast prevailed.*

Jacob went from being a commoner, to a prince in the eyes of Heaven. No one on Earth could see it. Jacob had no crown to wear, no royal sash, no imperial army, no palace. But Jacob knew who he was, and he carried himself with the confidence of royalty. It was audacious, unheard of, for a shepherd, an abomination, a Hebrew, to walk in before Pharaoh, put his hands on his head, and pronounce a blessing over him. This would be like a vagrant trying to touch and bless the

President of the United States! But Pharaoh let him, and no one stopped him.

There is enough that could be said here for an entire message in itself, maybe even a series of messages. But let me just give you a couple of quick thoughts on it:

The outward appearance doesn't usually tell the whole story.

Looking at it, the clothes, the living arrangements, the possessions, Pharaoh seemed to be by far the greater of the two. But the Bible is clear that the less is blessed of the greater. Jacob was the greater of the two.

You may not have a place to call your own, a car that shines, or a job that anyone else wants, but if you are a born-again child of God, you are greater than Bill Gates, with all of his billions, will ever be.

Our gratitude should not be just to the saved.

Pharaoh was not a Hebrew; he did not worship Jehovah God. He was lost. But he was also kind, at least to the family of Joseph. Jacob recognized that kindness and turned around and blessed Pharaoh for it.

I despise ingratitude. On July 8, 2008, a very well-fed woman came up to the new church, walked in, and announced to my wife that she was there for some gas money and food money. My wife said, "I'm sorry, we can't help you with that." The woman replied, "But I'm on empty!" My wife said, "I'm so sorry. We can't give you any money, but I just bought some snacks for our workers, you're welcome to a snack if you would like." That woman walked to the table, and took two, not two snacks, two BOXES of snacks, and waddled out. And do you know the worst part? She never even said thank you. So, being the spiritual giant that I am, I began to pray. I prayed, "Lord, please let every single one of those snacks give that woman diarrhea..."

I despise ingratitude! But God's people sometimes get the idea that we are only to be grateful to one another. Oh no, friend. In fact, it might be better to be grateful to the lost because the saved are already saved. If we are ungrateful when a lost person deserves our gratitude, what are the odds that they will ever be saved?

In September of 2007, we went on vacation to Myrtle Beach. We took a day and went to the Wacatee Zoo. It is a unique zoo, almost like something from the 1970's, with most of the animals in rickety pens with gates that can be opened. You can actually buy bags of feed and feed the animals.

One animal that we stopped to feed was a big black pig. My son, Caleb, especially enjoyed feeding that pig. But right in the middle of him doing something nice for that pig, the pig stuck its big snout out between the bottom of the gate and fence and bit him on the foot! That pig really bit him hard and hurt him pretty good.

A lot of Christians are like that big black pig; people do nice things for us and we turn around and bite them. Whether a person is lost or saved, if they deserve your gratitude, give it.

The Bread that Took Twenty Years to Bake
Genesis 47:11 *And Joseph placed his father and his brethren, and gave them a possession in the land of Egypt, in the best of the land, in the land of Rameses, as Pharaoh had commanded.* **12** *And Joseph nourished his father, and his brethren, and all his father's household, with bread, according to their families.*

Rameses was the capital of Goshen, which is why it is mentioned here. Joseph had his family settle down in that lush, fertile place, and verse 12 says that he nourished them all with bread. Most of the time bread takes two hours or so to bake, in this case it took twenty years. When he was just a teenager, his brothers sold him into slavery. He ended up in Egypt, became the second in command, was reunited with his family due to a famine, and now he is nourishing them with bread. I can't help but be struck by a poignant memory here:

Genesis 37:23 *And it came to pass, when Joseph was come unto his brethren, that they stript Joseph out of his coat, his coat of many colours that was on him;* **24** *And they took him, and cast him into a pit: and the pit was empty, there was no water in it.* **25** *And they sat down to eat bread...*

Tired, hungry, and scared, Joseph was in a pit, while his brothers ate their lunch on the outside of it. That would be hard to ever forgive. But twenty-some years later, when Joseph could have cast them into a pit and eaten his lunch, he instead chose to feed all of them. In other words, he returned good for evil. How very Scriptural:

1 Peter 3:8 *Finally, be ye all of one mind, having compassion one of another, love as brethren, be pitiful, be courteous:* **9** *Not rendering evil for evil, or railing for railing: but contrariwise blessing; knowing that ye are thereunto called, that ye should inherit a blessing.*

Romans 12:19 *Dearly beloved, avenge not yourselves, but rather give place unto wrath: for it is written, Vengeance is mine; I will repay, saith the Lord.* **20** *Therefore if thine enemy hunger, feed him; if he thirst, give him drink: for in so doing thou shalt heap coals of fire on his head.* **21** *Be not overcome of evil, but overcome evil with good.*

Sometimes, adults are like little kids. In Judith Viorst's children's book, *I'll Fix Anthony*, the younger brother complains about the way his older brother Anthony treats him:

> "My brother Anthony can read books now, but he won't read any books to me. He plays checkers with Bruce from his school. But when I want to play he says, "Go away or I'll clobber you." I let him wear my Snoopy sweatshirt, but he never lets me borrow his sword. Mother says deep down in his heart Anthony loves me. Anthony says deep down in his heart he thinks I stink. Mother says deep, deep down in his heart, where he doesn't even know it, Anthony loves me. Anthony says deep, deep down in his heart he still thinks I stink. When I'm six I'll fix Anthony... When I'm six I'll float, but Anthony will sink to the bottom. I'll dive off the board, but Anthony will change his mind. I'll breathe in and out when I should, but Anthony will only go glug, glug... When I'm six my teeth will fall out, and I'll put them under the bed, and the tooth fairy will take them away and leave dimes. Anthony's teeth won't fall

out. He'll wiggle and wiggle them, but they won't fall out. I might sell him one of my teeth, but I might not... Anthony is chasing me out of the playroom. He says I stink. He says he is going to clobber me. I have to run now, but I won't have to run when I'm six. When I'm six, I'll fix Anthony.³

Where does that kind of thing ever get anybody? Joseph could easily have "fixed" his brothers. In fact, he literally could have had them "fixed!" But instead, he thought ahead to the future instead of back into the past, and the result is that Israel came out of Egypt as a great nation, when they had gone in as just a little family.

What a church becomes through the years will be largely determined by whether or not we behave towards others as Joseph did towards his brothers. The bread may take a long time to bake, so let's go ahead and get started!

Chapter 20
The Jew that Made Egypt a World Power

Genesis 47:13 *And there was no bread in all the land; for the famine was very sore, so that the land of Egypt and all the land of Canaan fainted by reason of the famine.* **14** *And Joseph gathered up all the money that was found in the land of Egypt, and in the land of Canaan, for the corn which they bought: and Joseph brought the money into Pharaoh's house.* **15** *And when money failed in the land of Egypt, and in the land of Canaan, all the Egyptians came unto Joseph, and said, Give us bread: for why should we die in thy presence? for the money faileth.* **16** *And Joseph said, Give your cattle; and I will give you for your cattle, if money fail.* **17** *And they brought their cattle unto Joseph: and Joseph gave them bread in exchange for horses, and for the flocks, and for the cattle of the herds, and for the asses: and he fed them with bread for all their cattle for that year.* **18** *When that year was ended, they came unto him the second year, and said unto him, We will not hide it from my lord, how that our money is spent; my lord also hath our herds of cattle; there is not ought left in the sight of my lord, but our bodies, and our lands:* **19** *Wherefore shall we die before thine eyes, both we and our land? buy us and our land for bread, and we and our land will be servants unto Pharaoh: and give us seed, that we may live, and not die, that the land be not desolate.* **20** *And Joseph bought all the land of Egypt for Pharaoh; for the Egyptians sold every man his field, because the famine prevailed over them: so the land became Pharaoh's.*

21 *And as for the people, he removed them to cities from one end of the borders of Egypt even to the other end thereof.* **22** *Only the land of the priests bought he not; for the priests had a portion assigned them of Pharaoh, and did eat their portion which Pharaoh gave them: wherefore they sold not their lands.* **23** *Then Joseph said unto the people, Behold, I have bought you this day and your land for Pharaoh: lo, here is seed for you, and ye shall sow the land.* **24** *And it shall come to pass in the increase, that ye shall give the fifth part unto Pharaoh, and four parts shall be your own, for seed of the field, and for your food, and for them of your households, and for food for your little ones.* **25** *And they said, Thou hast saved our lives: let us find grace in the sight of my lord, and we will be Pharaoh's servants.* **26** *And Joseph made it a law over the land of Egypt unto this day, that Pharaoh should have the fifth part; except the land of the priests only, which became not Pharaoh's.* **27** *And Israel dwelt in the land of Egypt, in the country of Goshen; and they had possessions therein, and grew, and multiplied exceedingly.* **28** *And Jacob lived in the land of Egypt seventeen years: so the whole age of Jacob was an hundred forty and seven years.* **29** *And the time drew nigh that Israel must die: and he called his son Joseph, and said unto him, If now I have found grace in thy sight, put, I pray thee, thy hand under my thigh, and deal kindly and truly with me; bury me not, I pray thee, in Egypt:* **30** *But I will lie with my fathers, and thou shalt carry me out of Egypt, and bury me in their buryingplace. And he said, I will do as thou hast said.* **31** *And he said, Swear unto me. And he sware unto him. And Israel bowed himself upon the bed's head.*

Through the years, one of the most antagonistic nations to Israel has often been Egypt. Right now, Egypt is somewhat subdued towards Israel, but in 1948 when Israel was given back her homeland, Egypt was one of the nations that attacked her. On May 25, 1965, Egyptian President Gamal Abdel Nasser issued a statement that said, "The Arab national aim is the elimination of Israel." That strikes me as interesting, because if it were not for a little Jewish slave, Egypt as we know it would not exist today.

The Compilation of Property

Genesis 47:13 *And there was no bread in all the land; for the famine was very sore, so that the land of Egypt and all the land of Canaan fainted by reason of the famine.* **14** *And Joseph gathered up all the money that was found in the land of Egypt, and in the land of Canaan, for the corn which they bought: and Joseph brought the money into Pharaoh's house.*

After getting his family settled in Goshen, Joseph returned to the business at hand. There was still a famine ongoing, and it was a bad one. In a relatively short period of time, all of the land of Egypt and the land of Canaan were crippled by it. Matthew Henry said of this:

> "See here what a dependence we have upon God's providence. If its usual favours are suspended but for a while, we die, we perish, we all perish. All our wealth would not keep us from starving if the rain of heaven were but withheld for two or three years. See how much we lie at God's mercy..."[4]

As wealthy as the Egyptians were, famine still brought them to their knees. Both Egypt and Canaan were devastated, and it was only the foresight of Joseph that caused there to be food for the people to buy.

Here is a question for you. If there was a world-wide famine and the prices of the food that people did have shot through the roof, how long would it take you to go through every dollar you had just trying to keep you and your family alive? A week, a month, two or three? In a year's time, everyone in both Egypt and Canaan had spent every bit of money they had buying food from Pharaoh through Joseph. But the famine was still going on, and people were still hungry even after all the money was gone.

Genesis 47:15 *And when money failed in the land of Egypt, and in the land of Canaan, all the Egyptians came unto Joseph, and said, Give us bread: for why should we die in thy presence? for the money faileth.* **16** *And Joseph said, Give your cattle; and I will give you for your cattle, if money fail.* **17** *And* *they brought their cattle unto Joseph: and Joseph gave them bread in exchange for horses, and for the flocks, and for the cattle of the herds, and for the asses: and he fed them with bread for all their cattle for that year.*

How much would you give to stay alive? In this case, the people were willing to sell Pharaoh all of their livestock in exchange for food. Their money was now gone, their livestock was now gone, but they were alive.

Genesis 47:18 *When that year was ended, they came unto him the second year, and said unto him, We will not hide it from my lord, how that our money is spent; my lord also hath our herds of cattle; there is not ought left in the sight of my lord, but our bodies, and our lands:* **19** *Wherefore shall we die before thine eyes, both we and our land? buy us and our land for bread, and we and our land will be servants unto Pharaoh: and give us seed, that we may live, and not die, that the land be not desolate.* **20** *And Joseph bought all the land of Egypt for Pharaoh; for the Egyptians sold every man his field, because the famine prevailed over them: so the land became Pharaoh's.*

The second year referred to here means the year after they sold Joseph all of their livestock. The second year of the famine was back in Genesis 45, when Joseph's brothers first arrived. This is the sixth year of the famine itself. The Egyptians did better than most; it took them six years to be completely busted.

So they came back to Joseph and said, "We have no money, we have no more livestock, all we have left is our land and our bodies. Buy those and give us food. We will become servants to Pharaoh rather than die of starvation."

I am struck by the fact that according to verse 20, every one of the Egyptians went along with this. No one held out, no one said, "I'd rather die than be a slave." All of the land of Egypt became Pharaoh's.

Up until this time, though he was the most powerful man on earth, the power of Pharaoh was still limited. But now, with all property compiled into his possession, things were about to change.

The Consolidation of Power

Genesis 47:21 *And as for the people, he removed them to cities from one end of the borders of Egypt even to the other end thereof.* **22** *Only the land of the priests bought he not; for the priests had a portion assigned them of Pharaoh, and did eat their portion which Pharaoh gave them: wherefore they sold not their lands.*

Try imagining this with me. None of you own your properties anymore, and I am now going to make you leave your homes. The Taylors will be living in San Francisco. You Smiths, you will be moving to New Orleans. The Joneses, who are living in the family home, will now be in a trailer park in Alabama. The Blantons will be in a little apartment in Ramblewood. How do you like that?

Joseph was just doing his job, mind you. He was employed by Pharaoh, and he was doing what was best for his employer. It was more beneficial to Pharaoh to have the people spread out to work all the land than it was for him to have them all clustered together in one place. But from the other point of view, when these folks gave up their freedom for their food, things would never be the same for them. Again, I'm not bashing Joseph; he was doing his job. But this is an excellent opportunity to point out something that Americans have forgotten -- the government that provides for you possesses you!

"Hey, we're tired of paying high insurance premiums. Give us universal health care coverage!" The government that provides for you possesses you.

"Gas prices are too high. Let the government nationalize the gas industry, and give us what we need!" The government that provides for you possesses you.

"Food prices are going through the roof! Give us some program where we can just go into a grocery store, scan some government card, and get what we need! The government that provides for you possesses you.

"We can't afford our mortgages anymore. Which presidential candidate will promise to make my house payment for me?" The government that provides for you possesses you.

When Egypt became the provider for all of its citizens, it became the possessor of all of its citizens.

Genesis 47:23 *Then Joseph said unto the people, Behold, I have bought you this day and your land for Pharaoh: lo, here is seed for you, and ye shall sow the land.* **24** *And it shall come to pass in the increase, that ye shall give the fifth part unto Pharaoh, and four parts shall be your own, for seed of the field, and for your food, and for them of your households, and for food for your little ones.* **25** *And they said, Thou hast saved our lives: let us find grace in the sight of my lord, and we will be Pharaoh's servants.* **26** *And Joseph made it a law over the land of Egypt unto this day, that Pharaoh should have the fifth part; except the land of the priests only, which became not Pharaoh's.*

As far as we can tell from history and the Biblical record, this is the first "flat tax" in history! This is no doubt the simplest tax plan ever put in place. No matter who you are, no matter how little or how much you make, twenty percent of it belongs to the government, and the remaining eighty percent is your to do with as you will.

That is almost enough to make a body want to live in ancient Egypt! We haven't seen twenty percent taxes for decades! In local, state, and federal taxes, about sixty percent of all you make is taken by the government! And it still isn't enough for them. Every single year, they are going to do their very best to suck just a little more blood out of you. The thought of cutting back never occurs to them, unless it is them telling you to cut back.

Egypt managed to survive on a twenty percent tax rate, don't tell me our fat, bloated government couldn't do the same. This plan of Joseph made Pharaoh and the central government incredibly powerful. From this point, they went on to become a world superpower, so much so that Egypt is still around today, 3,500 years later. Yes, it was done at the expense of their freedom, but a Jew saved them from extinction and then made their government a powerhouse!

The Comfort of Privilege

Genesis 47:27 *And Israel dwelt in the land of Egypt, in the country of Goshen; and they had possessions therein, and grew, and multiplied exceedingly.*

Think back with me for just a moment. When the Egyptians got hungry, what was the first thing they gave up? Their money. When all of the money was gone, what did they give up next? All of their livestock. When all of their livestock was gone, what did they give up next? Their land and their freedom! They became indentured servants to Pharaoh. That famine devastated the Egyptians.

But how much money did the Israelites have to give up? How much of their livestock did they have to give up? How much of their land and freedom? While the Egyptians became poor in their own land, the Israelites, at least for that time, were living on easy street! Joseph fed them for free; they did not have to give up anything.

In later years, they would have it very, very difficult. But at least for a time, they were very comfortable and very well off. Was there any need for them to feel guilty over that? No, none at all. There was nothing dishonest going on; God was simply being very good to them. There will be many times that children of God have it very difficult, many times when it is hard to make ends meet, many times when we face outright persecution. But there will be other times when God allows us to be comfortable and maybe even well off. When we face bad times, be faithful and praise God anyway. When we face good times, enjoy them to the fullest and thank God for them.

The Concern of a Patriarch

Genesis 47:28 *And Jacob lived in the land of Egypt seventeen years: so the whole age of Jacob was an hundred forty and seven years.*

When Joseph was a baby, his daddy, Jacob, was there to take care of him. He went to work every day, put food on the table and clothes on his back. Jacob took care of his son for seventeen years, till Joseph disappeared.

When Jacob was old and frail, he was reunited with his son. And how long did Joseph take care of his old daddy, Jacob? Seventeen years. Joseph never forgot that his daddy took care of him, so when it was his turn, he cared for his daddy.

Young people, you need to know this. If your parents ever need you to take care of them, do it. I know it's weird to think of, but they once fed you while stuff dribbled down your chin, you may one day have to feed them while stuff dribbles down theirs. They kept your bottom clean, one day you may need to return the favor. Joseph was a man who honored his father.

Genesis 47:29 *And the time drew nigh that Israel must die: and he called his son Joseph, and said unto him, If now I have found grace in thy sight, put, I pray thee, thy hand under my thigh* **(this was their way of sealing a promise, much like a handshake today)**, *and deal kindly and truly with me; bury me not, I pray thee, in Egypt:* **30** *But I will lie with my fathers, and thou shalt carry me out of Egypt, and bury me in their buryingplace. And he said, I will do as thou hast said.* **31** *And he said, Swear unto me. And he sware unto him. And Israel bowed himself upon the bed's head.*

There is nothing funny about death, but I have got to tell you, the whole "funeral experience" can often be really interesting for the living.

Sometime back I was called on to assist in the funeral of a woman whose child we used to pick up on our bus. When the director of the funeral home called me, I could tell from the strained sound of his voice that things were not going well. I got cleaned up the next day and got over there, and he met me. He said, "If cussing would bring somebody back from the dead, that woman would be alive today, because her mother has spent two days cussing me for all I'm worth. She didn't like the way we did her hair or her clothes, she didn't like the casket or the casket spray, she is drunk as a skunk, and she doesn't like anything!"

Next day at the graveside, we read the Scripture and prayed. At the close of that, the mortician customarily makes his way round to the family under the tent, and tells them they can stay as long as they like. But on this occasion, having once again that day been cursed repeatedly, he went to the mother, and said curtly, "This concludes our service," and walked away!

Now, momma was right in front of the casket, and her "boy," a giant redneck biker dude was with her. He tried to get her to stand and leave. He got her up, but that is when she went berserk. She started screaming, "Don't put my baby in that hole, don't put my baby in that hole!"

What happened next though nearly made me blow a circuit trying not to laugh at such an inappropriate time. She screamed again, "Don't put my baby in that hole, don't put my baby in that hole!" and the biker son shouted out, "Well whar ya want us to put er, mommer, we gotta go!"

I have been at funerals where the family was split up into the two sides of the family, feuding like the Hatfields and McCoys.

And then there are those rare, rare funerals of wicked people where someone actually tells the truth. A funeral a few years ago in Georgia made the news. A wicked, wicked man had died, and as usual, his family brought him in for a big church funeral, expecting the preacher to preach him into Heaven. But not on this day. On this day, the preacher stood before the assembled family and said, "This man was a drunk, a worthless bum, a violent man with a filthy mouth, who had no regard for God. This man is in Hell right now, and that's where all of you are going if you don't get right with God!" The family dragged him out and beat him up! But I bet it was worth it.

But one of the more interesting things you often have to deal with in funerals is where someone will be buried. Several years back, I was asked to help in a funeral of an ornery old man. I agreed. The funeral was to be held in a nearby funeral home, the burial was to be "just up the road." Friends, I learned a valuable lesson that day. Always make people be very specific about where "just up the road" is. In this case, just up the road was an hour and forty-five minutes away, in a place so remote that I got lost coming back!

Dana has asked me where I want to be buried. I told her not to bury me, just stuff me and put me in a corner of the living room, holding a Bible in one hand, and pointing with the other.

Jacob had it good in Egypt. Because of Joseph, he and his family were well treated, and had not only the best in life, but the option to have the very best in death as well. May I point out to you that whenever elaborate tombs, with jewel encrusted mummies are found, they are found in Egypt! You just don't find that kind of thing anywhere in Israel.

But Jacob wanted to make very sure of one thing while he still could: he wanted to be buried in Israel, in Hebron, in the same place as Abraham and Isaac.

Jacob will not die till the end of chapter forty nine, and this study is about Joseph, not Jacob. But I do want to focus in on one aspect of this right now, as it pertains to Joseph and his father Jacob. For all of the greatness of Joseph, and for all the greatness of Egypt that Joseph was responsible for, Jacob taught Joseph a valuable lesson here. No matter how comfortable things are, get back to where you are supposed to be! God never intended for Israel to stay in Egypt forever, he intended for them to have Canaan. Jacob wanted to get back there as quickly as possible, even if it meant that his family would have to carry and bury him there.

So when Jacob gave these instructions, let me tell you what it was designed to accomplish. Number one, Jacob didn't even want his old dead body staying in Egypt, no matter how good they had it there. But number two, when the family went up out of Egypt to bury him later on, they were going to be feasting their eyes on Canaan again. They were going to be smelling the sweet air of the Promised Land again. They would hear the old familiar sounds again, the roaring of the Jordan, the lapping waves of the Dead Sea. Their feet would be on the same pathway that Abraham and Isaac had walked. Jacob's burial would stir their minds once more with a longing for Canaan. His death would cause them to look back at Egypt and say, "It's nice, but no matter how long we're there, we need to remember that it isn't home."

I just wonder, Mom, Dad, Grandma, Grandpa, will your death give your kids a longing for Heaven? I am at a lot of funerals where preachers will speak and family members will go on and on about the life of a person, and how nice they were **here**, and how good they made things for others **here**, but I notice that they are not able to say much that will make their families long for **There**.

Oh how much better it is when a family can stand and say, "Grandpa loved God. Look, here's his old Bible that we all saw him read night after night. Look at all these tear-stained pages. Look in the front cover at all of our names, his prayer list."

Oh, how much better it is when a preacher can stand and say, "Folks, your mama was the godliest woman I have ever known. She accepted Christ as her Savior many years ago, she was faithful to church every time the doors were open, she won souls, she prayed, your mama really is in Heaven!"

How much better is it when a parent can say, "I miss my girl, but I tell you what, she was ready to go. She always seemed to have one foot in Glory anyway. She was hungry for the things of God, she dressed modest to please Jesus, she kept herself pure, she had a sweet spirit, she loved Jesus more than anything in this world, and now she's with Him."

Jacob gave instructions for his funeral that would point his family towards home. The son made Egypt a world power, but the daddy made home something to long for.

Chapter 21
Daddy's Hands

Genesis 48:1 *And it came to pass after these things, that one told Joseph, Behold, thy father is sick: and he took with him his two sons, Manasseh and Ephraim.* **2** *And one told Jacob, and said, Behold, thy son Joseph cometh unto thee: and Israel strengthened himself, and sat upon the bed.* **3** *And Jacob said unto Joseph, God Almighty appeared unto me at Luz in the land of Canaan, and blessed me,* **4** *And said unto me, Behold, I will make thee fruitful, and multiply thee, and I will make of thee a multitude of people; and will give this land to thy seed after thee for an everlasting possession.* **5** *And now thy two sons, Ephraim and Manasseh, which were born unto thee in the land of Egypt before I came unto thee into Egypt, are mine; as Reuben and Simeon, they shall be mine.* **6** *And thy issue, which thou begettest after them, shall be thine, and shall be called after the name of their brethren in their inheritance.* **7** *And as for me, when I came from Padan, Rachel died by me in the land of Canaan in the way, when yet there was but a little way to come unto Ephrath: and I buried her there in the way of Ephrath; the same is Bethlehem.* **8** *And Israel beheld Joseph's sons, and said, Who are these?* **9** *And Joseph said unto his father, They are my sons, whom God hath given me in this place. And he said, Bring them, I pray thee, unto me, and I will bless them.* **10** *Now the eyes of Israel were dim for age, so that he could not see. And he brought them near unto him; and he kissed them, and embraced them.* **11** *And Israel said unto Joseph, I had not thought to see* *thy face: and, lo, God hath shewed me also thy seed.* **12** *And Joseph brought them out from between his knees, and he bowed himself with his face to the earth.* **13** *And Joseph took them both, Ephraim in his right hand toward Israel's left hand, and Manasseh in his left hand toward Israel's right hand, and brought them near unto him.* **14** *And Israel stretched out his right hand, and laid it upon Ephraim's head, who was the younger, and his left hand upon Manasseh's head, guiding his hands wittingly; for Manasseh was the firstborn.* **15** *And he blessed Joseph, and said, God, before whom my fathers Abraham and Isaac did walk, the God which fed me all my life long unto this day,* **16** *The Angel which redeemed me from all evil, bless the lads; and let my name be named on them, and the name of my fathers Abraham and Isaac; and let them grow into a multitude in the midst of the earth.* **17** *And when Joseph saw that his father laid his right hand upon the head of Ephraim, it displeased him: and he held up his father's hand, to remove it from Ephraim's head unto Manasseh's head.* **18** *And Joseph said unto his father, Not so, my father: for this is the firstborn; put thy right hand upon his head.* **19** *And his father refused, and said, I know it, my son, I know it: he also shall become a people, and he also shall be great: but truly his younger brother shall be greater than he, and his seed shall become a multitude of nations.* **20** *And he blessed them that day, saying, In thee shall Israel bless, saying, God make thee as Ephraim and as Manasseh: and he set Ephraim before Manasseh.* **21** *And Israel said unto Joseph, Behold, I die: but God shall be with you, and bring you again unto the land of your fathers.* **22** *Moreover I have given to thee one portion above thy brethren, which I took out of the hand of the Amorite with my sword and with my bow.*

Full circle, the hands of Jacob have come full circle...

In his youth, the hands of Jacob got him into trouble that lasted him for twenty years:

Genesis 27:15 *And Rebekah took goodly raiment of her eldest son Esau, which were with her in the house, and put them upon Jacob her younger son:* **16** *And she put the skins of the kids of the goats upon his hands, and upon the smooth of his neck:* **17** *And she gave the savoury meat and the bread, which she had prepared, into the hand of her son Jacob.* **18** *And he came unto his father, and said, My father: and he said, Here am*

I; who art thou, my son? **19** *And Jacob said unto his father, I am Esau thy firstborn; I have done according as thou badest me: arise, I pray thee, sit and eat of my venison, that thy soul may bless me.* **20** *And Isaac said unto his son, How is it that thou hast found it so quickly, my son? And he said, Because the LORD thy God brought it to me.* **21** *And Isaac said unto Jacob, Come near, I pray thee, that I may feel thee, my son, whether thou be my very son Esau or not.* **22** *And Jacob went near unto Isaac his father; and he felt him, and said, The voice is Jacob's voice, but the hands are the hands of Esau.* **23** *And he discerned him not, because his hands were hairy, as his brother Esau's hands: so he blessed him.*

Now, in his waning years, his hands are seen once more, this time with a different purpose and with different results.

After some years in Egypt, word was sent to Joseph that his aged father was sick. So Joseph gathered his own two sons born to him in Egypt, Ephraim and Manasseh, and went to see his father. When he arrived, Jacob began to speak:

Genesis 48:3 *And Jacob said unto Joseph, God Almighty appeared unto me at Luz in the land of Canaan, and blessed me,* **4** *And said unto me, Behold, I will make thee fruitful, and multiply thee, and I will make of thee a multitude of people; and will give this land to thy seed after thee for an everlasting possession.*

Jacob was hearkening back to his experience in Genesis 28. His likely purpose in so doing was to once again remind Joseph that they were only pilgrims in Egypt and must hand down from generation to generation the truth that they must one day leave.

In verse 5, Jacob issued an edict that was not customary for that day and age:

Genesis 48:5 *And now thy two sons, Ephraim and Manasseh, which were born unto thee in the land of Egypt before I came unto thee into Egypt, are mine; as Reuben and Simeon, they shall be mine.*

The grandsons of Jacob, the sons of Joseph, would be regarded as sons, equal in privilege to Joseph and all of his brothers. Succeeding history proved that to be correct, as Ephraim and Manasseh became two tribes, and, in fact, two of the most prominent tribes in Israel.

After having spoken of Ephraim and Manasseh, poor-sighted Jacob found that they were present in the room with him.

Genesis 48:8 *And Israel beheld Joseph's sons, and said, Who are these?* **9** *And Joseph said unto his father, They are my sons, whom God hath given me in this place. And he said, Bring them, I pray thee, unto me, and I will bless them.* **10** *Now the eyes of Israel were dim for age, so that he could not see. And he brought them near unto him; and he kissed them, and embraced them.* **11** *And Israel said unto Joseph, I had not thought to see thy face: and, lo, God hath shewed me also thy seed.* **12** *And Joseph brought them out from between his knees, and he bowed himself with his face to the earth.*

Jacob called for Joseph to bring them to him, so that he could bless them. Once again, this was a full circle experience for Jacob. He doubtless thought back a great many years, when he deceived his own blind father in order to receive the blessing that by custom would go to Esau. Now it was his turn to deliver a blessing, this time to two of his grandchildren.

Genesis 48:13 *And Joseph took them both, Ephraim in his right hand toward Israel's left hand, and Manasseh in his left hand toward Israel's right hand, and brought them near unto him.* **14** *And Israel stretched out his right hand, and laid it upon Ephraim's head, who was the younger, and his left hand upon Manasseh's head, guiding his hands wittingly; for Manasseh was the firstborn.* **15** *And he blessed Joseph, and said, God, before whom my fathers Abraham and Isaac did walk, the God which fed me all my life long unto this day,* **16** *The Angel which redeemed me from all evil, bless the lads; and let my name be named on them, and the name of my fathers Abraham and Isaac; and let them grow into a multitude in the midst of the earth.* **17** *And when Joseph saw that his father laid his right hand upon the head of Ephraim, it displeased him: and he held up his father's hand, to remove it from Ephraim's head unto Manasseh's head.*

Joseph, the younger who had been blessed above all of his elders, brought his own children in the traditional way, for the elder to be blessed above the younger. Jacob his father, who had been blessed rather than his older brother Esau, wittingly guided his hands cross-ways so that his right hand settled on the head of the younger, and his left hand settled on the head of the older. Joseph, verse 17 said, was displeased, and he demonstrated that displeasure by trying to physically remove and reset the hands of his own father!

How often are we as children of God guilty of that very thing, trying to "remove and reset" the hands of God in the way that we think they should go?

Genesis 48:18 *And Joseph said unto his father, Not so, my father: for this is the firstborn; put thy right hand upon his head.* **19** *And his father refused, and said, I know it, my son, I know it: he also shall become a people, and he also shall be great: but truly his younger brother shall be greater than he, and his seed shall become a multitude of nations.* **20** *And he blessed them that day, saying, In thee shall Israel bless, saying, God make thee as Ephraim and as Manasseh: and he set Ephraim before Manasseh.*

Joseph deserves a great deal of credit here, just as he did in every other instance recorded of him. When his father refused to move his hands, Joseph uttered no further protest. He realized that the only one who had the right to move the father's hands was the father.

Chapter 22
Of Bones and Burials

Genesis 50:1 *And Joseph fell upon his father's face, and wept upon him, and kissed him.* **2** *And Joseph commanded his servants the physicians to embalm his father: and the physicians embalmed Israel.* **3** *And forty days were fulfilled for him; for so are fulfilled the days of those which are embalmed: and the Egyptians mourned for him threescore and ten days.* **4** *And when the days of his mourning were past, Joseph spake unto the house of Pharaoh, saying, If now I have found grace in your eyes, speak, I pray you, in the ears of Pharaoh, saying,* **5** *My father made me swear, saying, Lo, I die: in my grave which I have digged for me in the land of Canaan, there shalt thou bury me. Now therefore let me go up, I pray thee, and bury my father, and I will come again.* **6** *And Pharaoh said, Go up, and bury thy father, according as he made thee swear.* **7** *And Joseph went up to bury his father: and with him went up all the servants of Pharaoh, the elders of his house, and all the elders of the land of Egypt,* **8** *And all the house of Joseph, and his brethren, and his father's house: only their little ones, and their flocks, and their herds, they left in the land of Goshen.* **9** *And there went up with him both chariots and horsemen: and it was a very great company.* **10** *And they came to the threshingfloor of Atad, which is beyond Jordan, and there they mourned with a great and very sore lamentation: and he made a mourning for his father seven days.* **11** *And when the inhabitants of the land, the Canaanites, saw the mourning in the floor of Atad, they* *said, This is a grievous mourning to the Egyptians: wherefore the name of it was called Abelmizraim, which is beyond Jordan.* **12** *And his sons did unto him according as he commanded them:* **13** *For his sons carried him into the land of Canaan, and buried him in the cave of the field of Machpelah, which Abraham bought with the field for a possession of a buryingplace of Ephron the Hittite, before Mamre.* **14** *And Joseph returned into Egypt, he, and his brethren, and all that went up with him to bury his father, after he had buried his father.* **15** *And when Joseph's brethren saw that their father was dead, they said, Joseph will peradventure hate us, and will certainly requite us all the evil which we did unto him.* **16** *And they sent a messenger unto Joseph, saying, Thy father did command before he died, saying,* **17** *So shall ye say unto Joseph, Forgive, I pray thee now, the trespass of thy brethren, and their sin; for they did unto thee evil: and now, we pray thee, forgive the trespass of the servants of the God of thy father. And Joseph wept when they spake unto him.* **18** *And his brethren also went and fell down before his face; and they said, Behold, we be thy servants.* **19** *And Joseph said unto them, Fear not: for am I in the place of God?* **20** *But as for you, ye thought evil against me; but God meant it unto good, to bring to pass, as it is this day, to save much people alive.* **21** *Now therefore fear ye not: I will nourish you, and your little ones. And he comforted them, and spake kindly unto them.* **22** *And Joseph dwelt in Egypt, he, and his father's house: and Joseph lived an hundred and ten years.* **23** *And Joseph saw Ephraim's children of the third generation: the children also of Machir the son of Manasseh were brought up upon Joseph's knees.* **24** *And Joseph said unto his brethren, I die: and God will surely visit you, and bring you out of this land unto the land which he sware to Abraham, to Isaac, and to Jacob.* **25** *And Joseph took an oath of the children of Israel, saying, God will surely visit you, and ye shall carry up my bones from hence.* **26** *So Joseph died, being an hundred and ten years old: and they embalmed him, and he was put in a coffin in Egypt.*

What a journey the life of Joseph was! He started out as the son that his father never thought he would have, a boy from the womb of Jacob's dear wife, Rachel. He was so loved by his father, and as a result, so hated by his other ten brothers. He was the possessor of the precious many-colored coat, and the recipient of prophetic dreams from God himself, dreams that later came to be in exact fashion.

He was also a victim. His own flesh and blood, his brothers, determined to kill him. In the end, they settled for stripping him of his coat of many colors, casting him into a pit, eating their meal while he begged for mercy from below them, selling him into slavery in a foreign land, and letting his father think he was dead.

But Joseph was also a blessed individual. He kept his character, and God continued to honor him, even as a slave in Egypt. Potiphar's wife tried to get him to sleep with her, and knowing it was wrong, he refused. So, when she was scorned in her own mind by Joseph running out of the house and leaving his coat behind to escape, she accused him of attempted rape, and had him thrown into prison. While there, God elevated him again, and he became the one in charge of the prison. God so arranged things that he was given the opportunity to interpret two dreams, one for the chief butler, and one for the chief baker, both of whom had been imprisoned. Two years later he found himself standing before the Pharaoh himself, interpreting a dream for him. Everything after that was an absolute whirlwind. In the blink of an eye, Joseph went from a prisoner to the second most powerful man on earth. He was the man with the plan for saving Egypt and the rest of the world from an incredible famine. It was that famine that brought ten very familiar faces before Joseph. They were older, more wrinkled and care-worn, but unmistakable, nonetheless. They didn't recognize him, but he recognized them. And he used that to a great, great advantage. He imprisoned Simeon and demanded that if they ever wanted to see him again and if they wanted so much as another mouthful of food, they would bring their youngest brother Benjamin, who they did not know was also his baby brother, back to Egypt with them. It took them a while to convince daddy Jacob, but when hunger finally got the best of them, they did just that.

When they got back, they didn't just get food, they got their money back, they got Simeon, and they got a wonderful meal and good fellowship in the house of Joseph. They left there feeling like the weight of the world was off their shoulders. How reassuring must it have been to think that if they ever needed anything, the second in command of all Egypt was now a friendly acquaintance.

That feeling of bliss was short lived. Not long after they left for home, the steward of Joseph caught up with them and accused them of stealing Joseph's "magic silver cup." He then searched their bags and found the cup (which he himself had planted) in Benjamin's bag. At that moment, their whole world fell apart. Joseph let them know that he would be keeping Benjamin as a slave and the rest of them were free to go.

It was at that moment that one of the brothers finally showed some character. Judah stepped to the forefront, and offered to stay as a slave instead of Benjamin. It was that great act of selflessness that finally broke Joseph out of his disguise and caused one of the greatest reunions in all of history. The entire family was in Egypt within a matter of days, and Joseph nourished them there. They rode out the famine in the lovely portion of Egypt known as Goshen, and they prospered while others around them were selling their lands, livestock, and finally their freedom to Pharaoh just to stay alive.

There came a day when Jacob was about to die, and he called all of his sons to him. Joseph brought his own two sons, Ephraim and Manasseh, and Jacob gave them the birthright that Reuben lost due to his wicked sin. He then pronounced prophecies of what these boy's tribes would be like way out into the future, and every single one of them came true. One cannot see all of this and fail to realize that there truly is much more to Joseph than just the many colored coat.

The Father's Burial

Genesis 50:1 *And Joseph fell upon his father's face, and wept upon him, and kissed him.*

In the last verse of chapter 49, Jacob, Joseph's father, died. Now we see all of the emotion just pouring out of Joseph. His daddy was old, he had long since ceased to be able to go and do, but he was still daddy, and Joseph loved him. They had been separated since Joseph was seventeen years old, reunited for seventeen years, and now Daddy Jacob was gone.

Genesis 50:2 *And Joseph commanded his servants the physicians to embalm his father: and the physicians embalmed Israel.*

Embalming was absolutely common to the Egyptians, but absolutely uncommon to the Israelis. Jacob may very well have been the first Jew ever to be embalmed. And in this case, it was going to be necessary, because Jacob while he was alive had commanded his family to take his body back to Canaan for burial. That body wouldn't have made it half a day in the heat of the desert without becoming bloated and unbearable.

All of those are simple, physical facts. But what is said next is something special.

Genesis 50:3 *And forty days were fulfilled for him; for so are fulfilled the days of those which are embalmed: and the Egyptians mourned for him threescore and ten days.*

The embalming process took forty days. That was normal. But what was not normal was for Egyptians to spend seventy days mourning for a Jew! Remember what we have already learned, that Jews in general and shepherds in particular were an abomination to the Egyptians. They would not even sit down at the same table with them. Yet here are the Egyptians, mourning and weeping for Joseph's old daddy. I'll say more about that in just a bit.

Genesis 50:4 *And when the days of his mourning were past, Joseph spake unto the house of Pharaoh, saying, If now I have found grace in your eyes, speak, I pray you, in the ears of Pharaoh, saying,* **5** *My father made me swear, saying, Lo, I die: in my grave which I have digged for me in the land of Canaan, there shalt thou bury me. Now therefore let me go up, I pray thee, and bury my father, and I will come again.* **6** *And Pharaoh said, Go up, and bury thy father, according as he made thee swear.*

Joseph sent word to Pharaoh, who was still his boss, asking for permission to go to Canaan and bury his father. Pharaoh gave permission. All of this is normal and customary. But once again, what happened next was absolutely uncommon and out of the ordinary.

Genesis 50:7 *And Joseph went up to bury his father: and with him went up all the servants of Pharaoh, the elders of his house, and all the elders of the land of Egypt,*

A few verses ago, we observed how the Egyptians mourned seventy days for Joseph's old daddy, Jacob. But now they go even further. They put together a state funeral for him. Everyone who was anyone in Egypt, except for Pharaoh himself, left Egypt, and followed that old, dead body into Canaan for burial. Once again, let's keep going and I'll say more about this in just a bit.

Genesis 50:8 *And all the house of Joseph, and his brethren, and his father's house: only their little ones, and their flocks, and their herds, they left in the land of Goshen.* **9** *And there went up with him both chariots and horsemen: and it was a very great company.* **10** *And they came to the threshingfloor of Atad, which is beyond Jordan, and there they mourned with a great and very sore lamentation: and he made a mourning for his father seven days.*

Just inside the borders of the Promised Land, the whole assembly stopped for seven days, and they all sat and mourned and moaned and wept and wailed during that week. It is described here as a great and very sore lamentation. You could expect that of family. But look at the next verse:

Genesis 50:11 *And when the inhabitants of the land, the Canaanites, saw the mourning in the floor of Atad, they said, This is a grievous mourning to the Egyptians: wherefore the name of it was called Abelmizraim* **(the mourning of the Egyptians)***, which is beyond Jordan.*

Were there family members, Jews, right there mourning over Jacob? Yes. But there were so many Egyptians there mourning that when the inhabitants of the land looked at it, they said this is a grievous mourning to the Egyptians!

Keep holding that thought; let's look a little further.

Genesis 50:12 *And his sons did unto him according as he commanded them:* **13** *For his sons carried him into the land of Canaan, and buried him in the cave of the field of Machpelah, which Abraham bought with the field for a possession of a buryingplace of Ephron the Hittite, before Mamre.* **14** *And Joseph returned into Egypt, he, and his brethren, and all that went up with him to bury his father, after he had buried his father.*

"All that went up with him" is separated from his brethren, his family, in this verse. The Egyptians went all the way to the grave site and were there for the burial of Jacob. Only then did they all turn around and head back into Egypt.

Now let me say some things about all of that. The Egyptians embalmed Jacob, the Egyptians mourned for him seventy days, the Egyptians, important men, powerful men, went into Canaan with the family. The Egyptians mourned right there inside the borders of Canaan for seven days, so many and so much so that the people said this is a great mourning to the Egyptians! The Egyptians made their way to the grave, and then and only then did they turn around and head for home.

For who? A king? No. A great ambassador? No. A powerful landholder? No. A wealthy man? No. Jacob was Jewish, old, poor, weak, and lived in a tent most of his life. This great state funeral was for a nobody. Here is the point, both Joseph and his daddy Jacob lived their lives in such a way that not only could the saved appreciate them but the lost could as well.

There are certain things that we cannot do, even though sinners would like us to. We cannot drink or cuss or do drugs or party or anything like that. We cannot condone sin, and we cannot stop preaching against it. But do you know what we can do? We can be kind... we can be honest... we can be compassionate... we can be consistent... we can be honorable.

Even lost people appreciate it when we pay our bills. Even lost people appreciate it when we show up in the hospital when they are sick or hurting. Even lost people appreciate it when we are patient and kind.

During our building project, I got one of the biggest blessings of my life. I was in Lowe's again, for about the ten thousandth time during those two and a half years. I went back into plumbing, and one of the ladies back there said, "You're the preacher, aren't you?" Before I could answer one of the other guys came by and said, "He sure is." She said, "I helped you with some sinks a couple of months ago. I remembered you because you were about the nicest customer I've ever dealt with." The guy chimed in and said, "He's the nicest customer we have, I always love seeing him come in."

When I left there, I called Dana and told her what happened, and I made this statement. "I remember all of the times I went in there in a hurry, dirty and nasty, sometimes irritated at how things were going at the building. I am so glad I was always able to smile and have a nice word for people. I'm glad that we didn't just build a building but also a reputation."

I would venture to say that some of those dear folks are lost. But why should I behave in such a way as to make them dislike me, Christ, and the church? Every one of us ought to live our lives in such a way that when we die, even the lost mourn for us.

The Fear of the Brothers
Genesis 50:15 *And when Joseph's brethren saw that their father was dead, they said, Joseph will peradventure hate us, and will certainly requite us all the evil which we did unto him.*

Let me tell you what is remarkable about this. What they did to Joseph was almost four decades before this! They are scared to death that they are going to have to pay the price for what they did almost four decades ago.

A guilty conscience is a hard thing to live with. If you want to lose sleep, live in sin. If you want to be suspicious of everybody around you, do something wrong. If you want to get bags under your eyes, try and hide wickedness. It will haunt you and rule you and ruin you.

A guilty conscience over sin has no expiration date. You can do wrong at sixteen and be nervous over it at sixty. Live right! Live right! Live right! If you want to have peace and joy and rest and calmness and assurance, live right.

Matthew Henry put it this way, "Those that would be fearless must keep themselves guiltless. If our heart reproach us not, then have we confidence both towards God and man."[5]

Live right!

Genesis 50:16 *And they sent a messenger unto Joseph, saying, Thy father did command before he died, saying,* **17** *So shall ye say unto Joseph, Forgive, I pray thee now, the trespass of thy brethren, and their sin; for they did unto thee evil: and now, we pray thee, forgive the trespass of the servants of the God of thy father. And Joseph wept when they spake unto him.* **18** *And his brethren also went and fell down before his face; and they said, Behold, we be thy servants.*

These guys are scared to death. While daddy Jacob was alive, they knew they would be okay. But now that he is gone, they fear that Joseph will kill them. They send for forgiveness and then come and ask for it personally, going so far as to say, "Little Brother, we are your servants."

Genesis 50:19 *And Joseph said unto them, Fear not: for am I in the place of God?*

This is one of the most refreshing verses in the Bible. It shows us a man in great power, which also has great humility. It shows us a man who didn't think that he was God. If these men were going to be put to death for their sin, Joseph figured that it was God's place to do it, not his.

But he's not going to let them off scot-free. They are going to be reminded of something:

Genesis 50:20 *But as for you, ye thought evil against me; but God meant it unto good, to bring to pass, as it is this day, to save much people alive.* **21** *Now therefore fear ye not: I will nourish you, and your little ones. And he comforted them, and spake kindly unto them.*

Joseph acknowledged their sin and their sinful intentions. It doesn't do people one ounce of good when they do wrong for us to pretend that they didn't!

But he also reminded them that our God is so big, so powerful, so all-knowing that He can make even our bad turn into something good.

Joseph ended by speaking kindly to them. That is another thing that is so good to learn. Many times when people do wrong and then truly apologize and try to make it right, we do the worst thing possible and "forgive them in a huff." You know what I mean, *"All right, I'll forgive you, this time, but I'm going to remember this and don't you ever do it again or else!"*

Not Joseph. Real forgiveness was sought and real forgiveness was given.

The Future of the Bones

Genesis 50:22 *And Joseph dwelt in Egypt, he, and his father's house: and Joseph lived an hundred and ten years.* **23** *And Joseph saw Ephraim's children of the third generation: the* *children also of Machir the son of Manasseh were brought up upon Joseph's knees.*

Joseph was sold into Egypt at seventeen years old. He lived there for the next ninety-three years. He went in as a teenager, then became a man, then became a husband, then became a father, then became a grandfather, then a great-grandfather, then a great-great- grandfather.

Genesis 50:24 *And Joseph said unto his brethren, I die: and God will surely visit you, and bring you out of this land unto the land which he sware to Abraham, to Isaac, and to Jacob.* **25** *And Joseph took an oath of the children of Israel, saying, God will surely visit you, and ye shall carry up my bones from hence.* **26** *So Joseph died, being an hundred and ten years old: and they embalmed him, and he was put in a coffin in Egypt.*

We talked about this recently, this thing of burials, and locations, and such. My mother-in-law has commanded that she not be buried in the rain. I want to be stuffed and stood up in a corner of the living room. Joseph commanded that the children of Israel pack up his bones and carry them with them.

But that was more than three hundred years before the Exodus. What was Joseph thinking? Did he actually believe that all those hundreds of years later, the future generations of his family would actually remember to do this?

Exodus 13:19 *And Moses took the bones of Joseph with him: for he had straitly sworn the children of Israel, saying, God will surely visit you; and ye shall carry up my bones away hence with you.*

You say, "But wait a minute preacher. Yes, they took his bones with them after that three hundred years, but then they ended up wandering around in the wilderness for forty years. Surely they just buried him somewhere along the way. I know they didn't actually haul him around that wilderness all that time!" You might just be surprised:

Joshua 24:32 *And the bones of Joseph, which the children of Israel brought up out of Egypt, buried they in Shechem, in a parcel of ground which Jacob bought of the sons of Hamor the father of Shechem for an hundred pieces of silver: and it became the inheritance of the children of Joseph.*

This to me is positively amazing. I can't get my kids to remember where they put their shoes thirty minutes after they took them off. Joseph got his family to remember to pack his bones along with them three hundred years after he died, then carry them around in the hot sun for forty more years, then bury them in the exact spot he told them to! What are the odds on that?

But here is the main point. Joseph wanted to make it all the way to the finish line. Egypt wasn't home, Canaan was home. He didn't want to get too comfortable; he didn't want to settle down in the wrong place. And by adopting this mind set, he sent a powerful message to his family three hundred years later. Every day that they wandered around the wilderness and whined about wanting to go back to Egypt, there would have to be at least one person who understood how important it was to go on into Canaan. Whoever had "bone duty" that day would be carrying around a tangible reminder that Egypt wasn't home, Canaan was home.

If that's what it takes, so be it. If I have to leave my bones here and have them in a sack for somebody to carry around when I'm gone, that's fine. Whatever it takes to remind people that this world is not our home, and we need to have our eyes fixed Heavenward instead of Earthward.

Colossians 3:2 *Set your affection on things above, not on things on the earth.*

Joseph had one final act to his life's play, and that was to become a tangible reminder not to settle down where they were, but to be pressing on towards home.

He is famous for the colored coat, but the colored coat was merely a point near the starting gate, there was so much more to his life than that. Joseph went from pampered son to the pit, to Potiphar's house, to the prison, to the palace, to providing for his reconciled family, to being planted right back in the Promised Land four hundred years later.

Notes

[1] Adam Clarke, <u>Commentary in Genesis</u>, (New York: Abingdon-Cokesbury Press), 244.

[2] Dr. Gary Collins in *Home Made,* 1985

[3] Judith Viorst, <u>I'll Fix Anthony</u>, (Aladdin Picture Books, 1988).

[4] Matthew Henry, <u>Commentary on Genesis</u>, (New York: Fleming H. Revell Company), 253.

[5] Ibid., 268.

www.ingramcontent.com/pod-product-compliance
Lightning Source LLC
LaVergne TN
LVHW051117080426
835510LV00018B/2095